THE LOST
PRAYER
OF JABEZ

THE LOST
PRAYER
OF JABEZ

Larry Pechawer

**A startling discovery now
changes EVERYTHING**

*David,
may all your
Produce Land
be green,
Larry*

The Lost Prayer of Jabez

published by MIREH Publishers

© 2001 by Larry Pechawer
Second Edition, revised and expanded, 2002
International Standard Book Number: 0-9716369-0-7

Cover Design by Mark Cole,
College Press Publishing Company

MIREH Publishers
P. O. Box 1376
Joplin, MO 64802

www.lostjabez.com

TABLE OF CONTENTS

More than two thousand years after his prayer was

recorded in the Hebrew Scriptures,

Jabez's words now appear in the bright

spotlight of the contemporary Christian scene.

Dr. Bruce Wilkinson has evoked an

incredible response from the Christian community

through his best seller, The Prayer of Jabez:

Breaking Through to the Blessed Life

(Multnomah, 2000).

With nine million copies sold and still counting,

this powerful little book has triggered

an avalanche of prayers, programs, critiques,

marketing strategies, and media attention.

Rarely has a religious book exploded

on the American scene with such force.

Meanwhile, however, a surprise has been lurking

in the shadows . . .

6

for more than two thousand years now.

This surprise lies buried

inside the ancient Hebrew text of Jabez's prayer,

hidden for all these years,

waiting to be brought to light.

Not a big surprise, as surprises go;

just a little one, nestled inside a rather obscure

verse - I Chronicles 4:10.

But by a remarkable turn of events, this verse has

suddenly become the most studied,

most prayed, most quoted, most talked about verse

in the entire Bible.

Now, information LOST for centuries

takes on new significance.

Now, tucked away inside the Prayer of Jabez,

we have a BIG surprise.

A surprise that changes EVERYTHING.

THE "POPULARIZED" VERSION OF THE PRAYER OF JABEZ

And Jabez called on the God of Israel

saying,

"Oh, that You would bless me indeed,

and enlarge my territory,

that Your hand would be with me,

and that You would keep me from evil,

that I may not cause pain!"

So God granted him what he requested.

I Chronicles 4:10

New King James Version

INTRODUCTION

Rest assured, this is not just another "anti-Jabez" work. We've had a rash of those lately. Frankly, some of the more recent ones (no names) are downright goofy. It's a case of the remedy (?) being worse, or at least more confusing, than the ailment.

The basic thesis of this present book is that **both** Bruce Wilkinson's *The Prayer of Jabez* **and** its critics are on the wrong track. How is that possible? How could we *all* be derailed on this issue? This book, *The Lost Prayer of Jabez*, provides the unexpected answer.

The first edition of *The Lost Prayer of Jabez* was published near the end of 2001. My initial uneasiness concerning the burgeoning Jabez phenomenon had heightened as more and more hype, products and paraphernalia emerged. All this over a rather obscure genealogical reference in Chronicles? Time to add my two cents, I thought. I just wasn't expecting how much different my conclusions would be from the mainstream.

I made a startling find ("The Discovery That Changes *Everything*"). My initial difficulties in translating Jabez's prayer from the Hebrew of I Chronicles 4:10 led to an unexpected conclusion. Ancient scribes and translators alike had made a fundamental mistake, one that has paved the way for our confusion and controversy now regarding Jabez and his prayer.

In essence, Jabez's original prayer has been *lost* for many centuries. How that could possibly be true is the subject of this book. A number of Hebrew scholars have now endorsed my findings (end of book). When people first encounter my rendition of what Jabez actually said, they are puzzled, to say the least. I try to help them through the issues and the facts. The goal of this book is to offer a compelling solution to the current Jabez "problem," while attempting to deal with some technical issues in a user-friendly way.

I'm not here to vilify anyone. Lots of web sites and publications can offer that fare for you. Frankly, the recent attacks on "poor" Bruce remind me of a free-throw contest in which the contestants are blindfolded. That's about as nasty as I'll get, so if you handled that comment okay you can proceed with confidence.

This second edition has undergone considerable changes from the first. Following the chapter entitled "The Discovery That Changes *Everything*" is a new chapter in which I provide a review of the arguments supporting my surprising conclusion. Also included are several additional arguments that I believe help make the case. A "Now What?" summary chapter then attempts to help readers assimilate my new interpretation of the Prayer of Jabez.

Once the case is made and third-party endorsements are provided, I close out the book with a substantial new chapter called "More About Jabez." This is provided for readers who wish to dig deeper into the Jabez saga. It's in three parts. First, in "The Prayer of Jabez Through the Ages," an in-depth survey of the treatment of this prayer throughout history is provided. To my knowledge, the material that I have assembled has never been seen before in connection with a study of the Prayer of Jabez. The most important early translations are analyzed, often with unexpected results.

Second, the ancient Jewish scholars are then researched in order to get their take on who Jabez was ("'Rabbi Jabez' and the Jewish Sages"). Considerable time is spent in explaining to the reader the nature of the "Oral Law" championed by the Rabbis (originally Pharisees). This sets the stage for encountering the Rabbinic texts. Those not familiar with Rabbinic interpretation (and most Christians aren't) will be in for a bit of a shock. Current extravagant claims regarding Jabez's significance don't compare with those in the ancient Jewish writings!

A brief section entitled "A Final Word for Specialists" closes out the book. In this, two important articles of a technical nature are discussed because of their significance for the interpretation of the Prayer of Jabez.

There are some lessons to learn from the current Jabez fiasco. Some evangelical leaders argue that preachers (and authors) are guilty today of "dumbing down" the gospel. The factors involved may be complex, but the overall feel one gets today is that there is some truth to this. When it comes to the "niceties" of Biblical history, theology, language and interpretation, we often function on a "need to know" basis in communicating with people. We won't get too "deep" unless they *really need to know* specifics involved. And *we* determine whether they "need to know."

Not all Christian leaders will welcome the contents of this book, because once the real issues that stem from today's Jabez fascination are identified, it becomes clear that our churches *do* need to know more. And if you're a church leader just starting in on my book, you probably will feel a little "ambushed" before you're done. But if you don't mind getting out of your comfort zone a bit, I think you'll enjoy the journey this book provides. May God bless you as you embrace with continued, even renewed, commitment the high calling of the teaching ministry of the church. Because of the Prayer of Jabez, your job just got a little harder.

THE JABEZ PHENOMENON

A new awareness of an obscure character in the Old Testament has emerged. The question Jabez . . . *who*? has now become Jabez! . . . *how*? Retrieved from the long lists of names in the Biblical book of I Chronicles, "Jabez" has become a code word for the pursuit of God's blessings. The Bible records that Jabez sought a blessing or gift from God and God honored his request (I Chronicles 4:10). So now the big question seems to be "How?" How can we receive the kind of response that God provided Jabez?

The runaway best seller by Bruce Wilkinson, *The Prayer of Jabez—Breaking Through to the Blessed Life*, clearly has struck a chord in the psyche of today's Christian community. Over nine million copies have been sold, along with the now customary accessaries: the prayer journal, the diary, the study guide (for just two verses?!), the leather-bound edition (aren't paperback and hardback enough?), the teenager edition, the women's version, pendants, calendars, shirts, and so on. I've heard that Jesus has even been taken out of the "Ichthus" fish and has been replaced by Jabez! We are talking about a burgeoning bonanza now approaching a quarter to a half *billion* dollars, in my rough estimation, especially when you consider the revenues generated by massive conferences and seminars. It is big business indeed.

One quickly picks up on the Jabez "lingo." We hear of people "Jabez praying." They may try the thirty-day "Jabez Experiment." If things go well they receive the "Jabez Blessing" and can expect to have a "Jabez Experience," which may involve various people with whom God will bring them in contact through "Jabez Encounters." As this happens they will have a sense that they indeed are on a "Jabez Journey" as they follow in the "Footprints of Jabez." (I saved my favorite for last.)

> *"Jabez" has become a code word for the pursuit of God's blessings.*

I have already noted that the big question on people's minds seems to be how *we* can receive the "Jabez blessing." That is certainly an interesting query, but it is *not* the question to which this work is devoted. Rather, **my basic question** speaks to the very *heart* of the Jabez "phenomenon." Simply put, it asks: **Has this**

Biblical passage even been correctly understood by the "Jabez Movement"? Or by anyone, for that matter?

The answer presented here is a resounding "No!" on several important levels. One level involves the improper application of Biblical truth—claiming that various portions of the Bible speak to issues and circumstances that in truth they do not. Another level concerns the choice of a popular translation that uniquely bolsters the Jabez "agenda" by a misleading rendering of the passage. A third level relates to the proper interpretation of the actual wording of the Biblical text. Some surprises are in store here, because much of the popularization of this passage was done without a careful examination of the text in its original language. Assumptions have been made that now need to be corrected.

The biggest surprise of all, however, awaits us on a fourth level. As I began to subject the most ancient form of the Hebrew Old Testament text to a detailed analysis, something unexpected surfaced. Something I wasn't looking for. Something that transforms the entire Jabez dialogue and debate. Something that changes EVERYTHING!

Don't get me wrong. Part of me is all for Jabez's meteoric rise to fame. Talk about an underdog! His life seemed to have no prospects for future acclaim. Buried back there in I Chronicles among the lists of tribal leaders and territories, no less, it's no wonder he has not exactly been a household name—until now. This climb to the top rivals Rocky Balboa's becoming heavyweight champion, or young Luke Skywalker's becoming a Jedi Knight! I guess the '69 Mets could fit in there too.

From what we read in Scripture, Jabez would seem to be worthy of some recognition (the fact that he's included in the Bible is a good start!). He was "honored among his brothers," and he fervently sought God's blessing in time of need. I Chronicles 4:10 ends by affirming that God answered his prayer (literally, God "brought about that which he had asked"). That ending statement is no doubt a big reason for the current Jabez phenomenon. Being blessed by God, especially in the precise way you *asked* to be blessed, sounds pretty good to most of us, doesn't it? "What's the secret?" we want to know. And there are those who would lead us to believe that there must be a lost key here of some kind. If only we can find the Jabez "formula." The closer we can emulate Jabez, the better our chances of experiencing what Jabez himself experienced. Or

> *Much of the popularization of this passage was done without a careful examination of the text in its original language.*

something like that. One thing is for sure, Jabez has never looked so good.

In a sense what follows serves as a corrective for what has become an almost bizarre glorification of this man—all done in the name of Biblical exposition, of course. But it has been built on an embarrassingly flimsy foundation. Dynamic application of the text to life is what is being sought by the "Jabez Movement." That's commendable. However, at some point the question needs to be asked: Has this all been taken from Scripture appropriately, or has it been a case of piling speculation upon speculation?

Then there comes the real "fly in the ointment," the fourth level of misunderstanding I spoke of earlier. Is it just possible that Jabez's prayer has been misunderstood all these many centuries? I am convinced that it has been.

Translations and commentaries alike have missed an important clue in the original Hebrew text that leads us to a startling new interpretation of what Jabez actually prayed. Some critical editions of the Hebrew text have hinted at this possible option for some time. Only trained specialists, however, have access to this information. And even they have not seen all the evidence mustered in a convenient form, until now.

The Jabez proponents certainly can't be faulted for missing this clue; it's buried pretty deep. But make no mistake about it. This clue, along with other evidence from the Biblical text, will introduce you to a different Jabez than many have recently come to know.

JABEZ OR JAZEB?

"Do you take off for spelling?" is one of my least favorite questions from college students. I translate that as "Don't expect too much!" I try to point out that careful spelling can really make a difference in distinguishing, say, Elijah from Elisha, or Jehoiakim from Jehoiachin. The early church, in discussing the deity of Christ, had it out over the difference between *homoousia* (same nature) and *homoiousia* (similar nature). These were terms used to describe the relationship between the Father and the Son. Spelling *back then* was a big deal, at least! Some students still don't seem convinced. Yet I continue to press my tireless campaign with my students, with my own two kids, with really anyone who will listen.

Believe it or not, part of the problem with the modern understanding of Jabez is a spelling problem! Once we understand what Jabez's name actually represents, then some of the current psychoanalysis of

> *Once we understand what Jabez's name actually represents, then some of the current psychoanalysis of this poor fellow may subside.*

this poor fellow may subside. It is commonly understood that Jabez's name means something like "pain," "he who causes pain," "he's a pain," or some such rendering. This is incorrect. It does not mean this, in spite of what everyone is saying. Let me explain.

First, the Bible does *not* say that Jabez's name has a meaning in the original Hebrew that has to do with "pain." Check for yourself. We might *assume* that his name did so since I Chronicles 4:9 states that his mother named him "Jabez" because she had such pain in the process of delivering him. But this assumption would be wrong. Some may describe what I'm about to explain as a technicality. If so, it is an important one. You see, the Hebrew root for pain, 'ATSAB, would produce a name YA'TSEB, or, in English spelling. "JAZEB." Mercifully, Jabez's mother did *not* give him *that* name, a name that would have clearly signified, "He's a pain!"

I can hear it now as "Jazeb" would have stood in line registering for the Judahite National Guard.

"What's your name?" "HE'S A PAIN, SIR!" (This gets glances from the guy next to him . . . .)

"You're saying that this guy over here is a pain?" "NO SIR, I AM!"

"You're a pain?" "NO SIR, *HE'S* A PAIN." "Forget about him. Who are you?" "HE'S A PAIN, SIR."

"He is . . ." "A PAIN, SIR."

"Him?" "NO, ME."

"Okay, good, we're back to you. And your name is . . .?" "HE'S A PAIN."

"Young man . . ." (Abbott and Costello, take it from here!)

But his mother didn't name him **"Jazeb."** Rather, she called him **"Jabez,"** a name which sounded similar, but which was quite distinct. In essence she transposed the last two letters of the Hebrew word denoting pain in naming her son. YA'TSEB thus became YA'BETS, or, in our English representation, "Jabez." The meaning of this particular Hebrew root is not agreed upon by Hebrew scholars. No clear connection exists with any known words.

> *Jabez had an unusual name (the only individual in the Old Testament so named), but not necessarily a humiliating one.*

In any event, Jabez's name sounded *similar*, but not identical, to the "pain" word. Thus Jabez had an *unusual*

name (the only individual in the Old Testament so named) but not necessarily a *humiliating* one. <u>It is at the very least a real stretch to depict Jabez as a man whose life was burdened by his moniker.</u>

Recent writers, however, have indeed portrayed him in this light. Take the words of Bruce Wilkinson:

> Only God knows for sure what caused the pain of this anguished mother. Not that it made much difference to young Jabez. He grew up with a name any boy would love to hate (*The Prayer of Jabez*, p. 21).
>
> Yet by far the heaviest burden of Jabez's name was how it defined his future (p. 21).
>
> A name was often taken as a wish for or prophecy about the child's future (p. 21).
>
> A name that meant "pain" didn't bode well for Jabez's future. Despite his dismal prospects, Jabez found a way out (pp. 21-22).

Jay Dennis has similarly opined:

> From his earliest memories Jabez could only remember a life defined by pain (*The Prayer Experiment*, Zondervan 2001, p. 36).
>
> All of his life Jabez lived with broken dreams and fallen rainbows. With a name the equivalent of "Major Disappointment," he no doubt felt inadequate and insecure and had every reason to fail dreaming big things for his life (pp. 93-94).
>
> We cannot know for sure, but given his name, his parents sound like they could have easily been a toxic influence in his life. Growing up, he undoubtedly faced ridicule by those who felt superior to him. Certainly there would have been those who meant well, but felt compelled to remind him how unlikely it would be for him to

make a significant mark on the world. Can't you imagine their discouraging—and probably less than discreet—comments?

"Poor thing...."

"Bless his heart...."

"His poor parents...."

"What are his chances?" (p. 116)

The above descriptions would seem to speak little to the actual situation of Jabez's life, especially when we understand the true nature of his name. The name "Jabez" might have conveyed a special sense for his mother, but there is no indication that others viewed it as a reason for ridicule, or that Jabez himself was emotionally affected by his label.

Quite the contrary is suggested by the words of verse nine: "Now Jabez was more honored than his brothers ...." Most of the recent translations give this sense. Four important translations, however, chose to render this instead as more "honorable": the King James Version, the New King James, the New American Standard Bible, and the New International Version. Each states that Jabez was more "honorable" than his brothers. All of these are excellent translations, of course, but in this particular instance they should be passed up in favor of the previously noted option— "honored," and not "honorable."

The exact same underlying Hebrew expression is used of the Canaanite chieftain Shechem in Genesis

34:19. But these translations do not translate the term as "honorable" there for a very good reason. He himself was *not* very "honorable," as his sexual violation of the Hebrew maiden Dinah made clear. In his case, his leadership position, not his moral disposition, was the point.

The four translations singled out above all render the meaning as "honored" in the Genesis 34 passage. I would contend that the same wording (NIKBAD ME'EKHAW, "more honored than his brothers") should be applied at I Chronicles 4 as well. Jabez's moral integrity can perhaps be argued from the fact that God honored his prayer, and also from the fact that he was looked up to by his brothers. The translation "honorable," however, goes too far in proclaiming a moral integrity that is merely implied in the Biblical text itself. Jabez was *honored* above his brothers, a noted and respected leader among them.

The use of Jabez's name to promote the idea of some special need or crisis in his life is simply not supported by the actual Scriptural account. Had his mom actually named him "Jazeb," that may have been a different story. But the name "Jabez" itself should have created no particular hardship in his life. As it was, Jabez's distress or "pain" was of a different nature, as we shall see.

JABEZ'S TRUE DESIRE

Now that Jabez's name has been cleared up, there is another critical question to address. What exactly did Jabez pray for? The spiritual profile of Jabez created by Bruce Wilkinson in his *The Prayer of Jabez* would lead us to believe a scenario in which Jabez desired to make something of his lowly, troubled life. Shackled with a name meaning "He's a pain" (which it *does not* mean), Jabez was ready for some transforming miracle in his life. He called out to God to grant him greater opportunity for service, greater influence, a greater stewardship of life, etc., etc. That's what "enlarge my territory" is supposed to mean.

But let's go slowly here before climbing upon an avalanche of speculation. I personally understand Jabez's desire for God to "enlarge his territory" (literally "border") to mean that Jabez wanted more . . . TERRITORY! Admittedly a simplistic approach, but what else is there really? Jabez sought the blessing of increased land and God granted that request.

The fact that God granted Jabez's request is, of course, a big reason for the fascination with this prayer. We'd like to know more about prayers that God grants. It's only natural. After all, that last assertion is likely the only reason why Jabez's life is focused on briefly by the Chronicler in the Old Testament. Jabez was more than just one of the many so-and-so's in the tribal list. We are not told about the others, but of Jabez we read that God answered *that* godly man's prayer.

I do assume that Jabez was godly, but really we know only two things for sure. One, he was honored above his brothers (not necessarily "more honorable" than them); and two, he earnestly sought God's blessing for his life. In this case, it was the blessing of increased land and the relief that would provide.

Based on this account we are being counseled by some that the key to being blessed is to *ask* to be blessed. Who knows, they ponder, how many blessings we have forfeited simply because we have failed to ask? The prayer of Jabez is being paraded as the new "model prayer" to follow. But surely this isolated request by Jabez is a slender thread on which to hang a

> Will *WWJD?*
> now become
> "What Would
> *Jabez* Do?"

theology of prayer or divine blessing. This is especially so in light of the "discovery" to be presented later.

Jabez's prayer has an emphatic tone. The Hebrew expression in this passage employs a special device to indicate strong petitioning. The main verb is supplemented by a special additional verbal form (which happens to be called an "infinitive absolute"). Literally we might say (but we *shouldn't* for the sake of meaningful translation), "O that blessing You would bless me," or "If blessing You would bless me." Instead we use the strengthening element "indeed" or "surely." "If you would indeed bless me" gives the thought nicely. Better yet, "If you would *only* bless me . . . ." Jabez's prayer possessed a sense of urgency about it, no question.

We may reasonably ask the question *why* Jabez earnestly desired more land. Two options come to mind, greed or need. We can safely rule out greed, it seems to me. That leaves us with need. In the next chapter we will talk about "Jabez the Farmer." For now we will just suggest that the desire for expanded territory was likely based upon the needs of his family and herds. Quality grazing land for livestock—without sufficient supply Jabez would indeed likely suffer "pain" or distress.

We now are being asked to believe that Jabez's prayer, "enlarge my territory," was primarily spiritually motivated, a desire to make his life count for God in a bigger way. This whole approach represents a fascinating

27

but definitely flawed interpretive scheme. What is first argued is that Jabez's request must be "spiritualized" as we seek to apply it to our own lives. We are told not to view this prayer as a proof text to seek material prosperity, but rather spiritual or ministry opportunities. That's fine as a suggested application of the text, I suppose, but even with this it is somewhat of a stretch.

But what is interesting is what comes next. The spiritual application extended to us is then "retrofitted" back to Jabez himself. Now it's *Jabez* who sought greater influence in his life. "Like Jabez," we should seek broader avenues of glorifying and serving our Lord. "Like Jabez," we should desire more ministry opportunities. *The spiritual application imposed upon us from the text has been smuggled back into the text itself.* ✓

> **"RETROFIT"** - *"to furnish with new or modified parts or equipment not available or considered necessary at the time of manufacture."*

Preachers have delivered sermons on the prayer of Jabez for years. But once Jabez is fully "retrofitted," his prayer no longer is merely an isolated prayer from which we might seek some spiritual application. Rather, it takes on the identity of a divinely crafted spiritual road map to follow. We just need to "be like Jabez."

But this is not a credible way to treat the teachings of Scripture, even when it's done in the name of furthering the growth and ministry of the church. Regardless of whether my new interpretation presented in this book be accepted, the "Jabez Movement" applications of the text of this prayer are fanciful and forced.

I am convinced that the closing words of the prayer have had an influence on the spiritualizing efforts of some. Here, according to the New King James Version, Jabez asks God to protect him from evil so that he "will not cause pain" to others. These last words serve to cast the entire prayer into "super spirituality" mode. The words "keep me from evil" are alleged to indicate Jabez's desire not to be led into temptation. He wants to eradicate sin from his life. Noble sentiments, but is this what Jabez actually prayed? The closing thought, "that I may not cause pain," speaks to Jabez's desire not to be a spiritual stumbling block to others—another lofty ideal. No wonder the logical jump is made to reinterpret Jabez's request for "enlarged territory" in more spiritual terms.

In light of what has just been said, then, it is important to realize that of all the many English translations, young and old, *the New King James Version is the only translation that understands the ending of the verse in this way.* Most understand the word RA'AH as "harm" or "calamity" rather than "evil" in the sense of "sin." According to the vast majority of translations, Jabez sought to be free from "disaster" or "harm" in his life, not "free from sin." More importantly, however, the words "that I may not *cause* pain" (New King James) are universally rendered outside of the New King James Version as something like "that I may not *suffer* pain." We're talking here about the King James, New International, New American Standard, New American (Roman Catholic), Revised Standard, New Revised Standard, New English, New Century, Amplified, Contemporary English, New Living, and the list goes on and on.

Without impugning motives let's just note well that much of the current Jabez "persona" is based on a solitary and, in my view, suspect translation. The Hebrew should be read something like "so as not to pain me," or better, "so that I will not be in distress." Jabez was asking God to keep *him* from pain or distress, not to enable him to keep from hurting *others*. This seems clear. Jabez's luster is fading just a bit, I'm afraid.

JABEZ THE FARMER

I think Jabez would have enjoyed the song "The Green, Green Grass of Home." He no doubt was a down-on-the-farm kind of guy. What else was there in earliest Israel? Before we start surmising that Jabez's desire for more "territory" had a deeper, broader meaning, we should take stock of the role that land played back then.

When I read through the accounts of the tribal leaders and their territories in the books of Joshua and I Chronicles, I am impressed by the attention to the everyday things of life and its sustenance. For example, we know that the Levites did not inherit a territory as such, but rather were given possession of forty-eight cities, the "Levitical cities," including six "cities of refuge." We read that the Levites were given these cities along with their pasture lands for their livestock. Like an ongoing refrain, all of the forty-eight cities are listed, each new city reference ending with the words "with its pasture lands" (I Chronicles 6:54-81; also Joshua 21:1-42). Joshua 21:41-42 then summarizes the whole situation:

The towns of the Levites in the territory held by the Israelites were forty-eight in all, together with their pasturelands. Each of these towns had pasturelands surrounding it; this was true for all these towns.

This provision fulfilled the requirements in the law of Moses to provide pasture land for each Levitical city. The dimensions specified in Numbers 35:1-5 involved a square surrounding each city measuring three thousand feet on each side. Pasture land for the flocks and herds was a big deal.

We should note that there are different terms in the Hebrew Scriptures for "pasture, pasture land." One term conveys the sense of the herd's "habitation" or possibly the shepherd's "destination" for the flock (Psalm 23:2). Another, the idea of "feeding ground" (I Chronicles 4:39). Here in Joshua 21 and I Chronicles 6, the term throughout denotes "cleared land."

Another song that comes to mind is the old classic "Don't Fence Me In." I'm not sure that Jabez would have connected as much with that one. The notion of "Land, lots of land . . ." may not have been as desirable as the right *kind* of land. Green, watered pasture land—now that's something to sing about.

Caleb's daughter Achsah, mentioned in Joshua 15:16-19, certainly felt that way. We remember Caleb as one of only two spies (along with Joshua) who gave a positive report concerning Israel's prospects for conquering the land of Canaan. Once individual tribes began the secondary phase of each tribe's conquest of assigned land, Caleb, now an energetic, ambitious eighty-five year old, asked to be given the hill country of Hebron (Joshua 14:10-15). Caleb was among the sons of Judah, as was Jabez. (The emphasis on Judah is understandable in light of Chronicles' interest in the royal line of David.) He offered his daughter Achsah in marriage to the man who captured the city of Debir (Kiriath-Sepher). Othniel rose to the challenge and won the girl (Joshua 15:16-17). Later Achsah rode up on her donkey, got off and asked daddy,

"Do me a special favor. Since you have given me land in the Negev, give me also springs of water." So Caleb gave her the upper and lower springs (Joshua 15:19).

The expression "do me a special favor" in the New International Version renders a Hebrew phrase that literally reads "Give me a blessing!" Sounds a bit like Jabez. In essence, Achsah wanted to guarantee that she had access to the kind of natural resources that would allow her estate to thrive. The springs would provide such assurance.

At the end of the very chapter in Chronicles containing the Prayer of Jabez, we read of the men of the tribe of Simeon seeking land, lush pasture land, for

33

their flocks. Gorgeous land. Land to kill for . . . literally! Let's allow Chronicles to tell the story:

> The men listed above by name were leaders of their clans. Their families increased greatly, and they went to the outskirts of Gedor to the east of the valley in search of pasture for their flocks. They found rich, good pasture, and the land was spacious, peaceful and quiet. Some Hamites had lived there formerly. The men whose names were listed came in the days of Hezekiah king of Judah. They attacked the Hamites in their dwellings and also the Meunites who were there and completely destroyed them, as is evident to this day. Then they settled in their place, because there was pasture for their flocks (I Chronicles 4:38-41).

Quite a fascinating account when placed next to Jabez's request of God earlier in the same chapter: "Enlarge my territory and may your hand be with me!" One thing becomes obvious. Quality, productive land was the object of desire for many in early Israel. It does not require speculation to contend that Jabez likely shared such aspirations. This becomes a significant clue in our search for the "lost" Prayer of Jabez.

JABEZ THE POET?

Jabez's credentials as a man of the land should not be questioned. But was he a man with a literary flair as well? Did his prayer have a poetic quality to it, or was it simply a narration of requests being made to God—something like a shopping list? As the prayer is popularly understood, there is not much poetic style evidenced. My later proposal, however, will significantly enhance the poetic nature of the prayer.

Unlike the poetry of English and many other languages, Hebrew poetry does not generally rhyme. If your Bible shows rhyming it is probably due to a creative translator! What Hebrew poetry does exhibit is *parallelism*, a balancing of terms or thoughts. This parallelism is the primary characteristic of Hebrew poetry.

Sometimes the balancing of thoughts involves similar phrasing (*synonymous* parallelism). Other times opposing ideas are expressed (*antithetic* parallelism). A more difficult, broader category is that of *synthetic* parallelism, in which one line supplements, qualifies, or enhances another. Let's look at examples of each.

Psalm 51:7 reads,
Cleanse me with hyssop, and I will be clean;
wash me, and I will be whiter than snow (synonymous).

Proverbs 14:11 says,
The house of the wicked will be destroyed,
but the tent of the upright will flourish
(antithetic; Proverbs is full of this kind of parallelism.)

Psalm 96:1 reads,
Sing to the LORD a new song;
sing to the LORD, all the earth (synthetic).

Other classifications have been done, but you've gotten the idea. Note that the example from Psalm 51 is from a prayer, David's famous petition to God following his sin with Bathsheba. Many prayers in Scripture contain poetic parallelism–Hezekiah's (Isaiah 36:14-20; 38:9-20); Joshua's (Joshua 10:12-13); Solomon's (I Kings 8); and of course the Psalms are full of such prayers. But did Jabez's prayer contain such poetic structure? As currently understood, not really. But stay tuned.

TRANSLATION TROUBLES

As I began to analyze the Prayer of Jabez in depth, my first reaction to the Hebrew text was, "Boy, this is tough. This shouldn't be so hard. What am I missing here?" I'll get to my major problem with the text in a minute. For the most part, the various English translations are in agreement with the basic thrust of the prayer. However, there are a couple of issues that they disagree on.

Was Jabez "*honored* from among his brothers" or "more *honorable* than his brothers"? I have already argued that the former is the case. The term "honorable" conveys more in English than the Hebrew necessarily expresses. Some of the more prominent modern translations have unfortunately gone with "honorable" here. The New International Version is one of them. Yet the (Niphal) participle form, NIKBAD, found here at I Chronicles 4:9, at Genesis 34:19, and at some fifteen other places in the Old Testament, is generally rendered "honored," not "honorable." Esteem given by others is what is conveyed. Jabez indeed may have been "honorable," but that's not what's being said here. *The translation "honorable" should be abandoned at I Chronicles 4:9.*

Another question is whether Jabez asked to be kept from "evil/sin" or from "harm/disaster." As you will soon discover, I am not too concerned about this particular issue, but the options do color the current debate. Based on earlier discussion, the best answer would seem to be "harm/ disaster." Jabez wished to be protected from any mishap or harm that would distress or "pain" him.

That leads us to the translation problem at the very end of the verse. Did Jabez ask to be kept *from* "pain," or did he ask that he might be kept from "paining" *others?* Well, another question needs to be asked. Is this really a translation problem at all? Let me repeat what I said earlier. No translation except the New King James Version conveys this latter, more spiritually-minded notion. Yet this is the rendering that has been chosen as the "official" Jabez prayer. Why? And, having chosen this rather suggestive reading, why doesn't Wilkinson's *The Prayer of Jabez* comment on it?

I think Kathy Callahan-Howell has it right in her letter to *Leadership* magazine when she writes, "So it seems to me Wilkinson chose the less selfish version to add to the book's appeal, but was afraid to focus on it since it's a weak translation" (*Leadership*, Fall 2001, p. 15).

But is it even remotely *possible* that this "maverick" rendering is correct against all the others? The answer is "Yes, it is possible," but the argument takes us too deep into the realm of Hebrew specialists. Be forewarned that I am about to present a translation option that NO English translation has ever adopted. Does that make me wrong? Opinions will differ on the answer to that question, no doubt.

In any case, the most likely, and, I believe, *necessary* understanding of the prayer is that Jabez himself does not wish to experience distress or "pain." My own translation will bear that out and will show it to be the only real possibility in the final analysis. "Pain me" represents a Hebrew infinitive with an object pronoun suffix attached. "Me" is the object of the "paining," not the subject doing the "paining," at least in this particular context. (Without going into more detail than would be helpful, I would just note that if the Hebrew pronoun suffix were a *subject* pronoun, therefore "my paining," we would almost certainly also find a stated direct object identifying *whom* he would not be "paining.")

We now arrive at the big problem in our English translations: what to do with the Hebrew verb 'ASAH in the phrase "keep me from harm." The expression "from harm" seems clear enough for now (MERA'AH, with "from harm" being preferred here over "from evil"). It's the KEEP ME that is puzzling. Everyone agrees that is what the verb *should* mean, but no one has convincingly shown *how* it can mean this.

This is the situation. The root 'ASAH has the general meaning of "do" or "make." By natural extension it often means "provide," "celebrate" (a festival), "prepare," "obey" (a command), "perform" and a host of other things, depending on the nature of the thing made or done. But none of the various possibilities help us here at I Chronicles 4:10. We need something like "KEEP from harm" or "DELIVER from harm" but no attested usage of the verb 'ASAH gives anything close to that. "Keeping"(doing) laws does not serve as a valid analogy. A verb signifying some form of protection is really demanded, and we just don't have it.

'ASAH never signifies "keep from" or "deliver from." Editors of one of our standard printed Hebrew Bibles placed the notation "crrp" in their footnote apparatus (suggesting that in their opinion the text has been "corrupted"). Some critics have suggested we emend or "correct" the text by changing just two letters, thus forming a new word meaning "deliver" and so giving us a reading "deliver from harm." That would solve the problem, right? Definitely *wrong* in this case for sure. Please note that by leaving the Hebrew letters *exactly as they stand*, we can arrive at a perfect solution. It's just not a solution anyone was expecting, including me!

Let me put this in the starkest terms possible. The Hebrew verb 'ASAH occurs *over 2,600 times* in the Old Testament, and NEVER with the sense proposed by our English translations here in

> *By leaving the Hebrew letters exactly as they stand, we can arrive at a perfect solution.*

the prayer of Jabez. Critics have wanted to emend or alter the text; our translations have chosen in a sense to *ignore* it! But that may soon change.

A good illustration of how unsatisfactory our current understanding of this prayer is comes from the earliest known translation of the Old Testament, the Greek "Septuagint" (often abbreviated LXX, so named because of the tradition that states the number of translators involved as being "seventy"). Produced several centuries before Christ, the Septuagint reveals an alternate understanding of the text. Apparently, "make from evil" did not grab those early translators either. Perhaps because of this, they developed an entirely different read on the passage. Two letters in the Hebrew script that can easily be confused are the "R" and the "D." This happens dozens of times in the LXX rendering of names, understandable since the true nature of many proper names could be lost over time. The Hebrew language did not represent vowels as a rule, so that would make the "name game" just that much harder. At the time the book of Chronicles was written, the two letters were virtually identical. Context is really the only sure guide in many cases. Since the phrase "make from harm" makes little sense, this passage was a good candidate for a facelift.

The LXX translators gave it one. Instead of reading MR'H (MERA'AH, "from harm"), they read it MD'H, which they took to signify MADDA'AH, meaning "knowledge." Well and good, although this would be the only time in the Hebrew Old Testament that the word is spelled this way (elsewhere simply MADDA'). Their take, then, was something like "and make me know that I will not suffer pain." An interesting request, isn't it? But there is not much to commend this understanding. Commentaries and translations have not taken it seriously. The point to be emphasized here, though, is simply that the LXX did not see 'ASITA MERA'AH, "make from evil," as a good option ('ASITA is a form of 'ASAH). Their instincts were right. Their remedy was not.

Before I finally share with you the discovery that changes EVERYTHING, a short Hebrew lesson is in order. This will make the reasoning behind my discovery clearer. Besides, Hebrew is *fun*!

HOW DO YOU SPELL HEBREW?

Before we come to the solution to our puzzle, we have to deal with the question, "How do you spell Hebrew?" The simple answer would be H-E-B-R-E-W!! The tougher answer deals with how ancient Hebrew scribes handed down the sacred text to future generations. This was done by them with an amazing degree of accuracy and faithfulness to the Scriptures they were seeking to preserve. The Hebrew text of the Old Testament we possess today underwent several stages in its development to arrive at its present final form. The information gained now in this quick overview will help us in better understanding what the original prayer of Jabez probably sounded like and meant.

The Hebrew language consists of twenty-two letters, all of which were originally consonants. In the earliest stages of Hebrew and related languages such as

Aramaic and Phoenician, no vowels were apparently indicated, only consonants. (The Phoenicians, Canaanites who lived along the Mediterranean coast of Palestine, are generally credited with developing the alphabet used in our Hebrew Bible. They also likely were the ones who transmitted it to the Greek culture and language. Our modern English alphabet ultimately derives from this same alphabet.) Writing without vowels created some ambiguity, as might be expected. Knowing the culture and immediate circumstances would be key in achieving full comprehension.

Let's try an illustration using English without vowels: KNG GRG WS M FVRT *NGLSH RLR (The * indicates that the word begins with a vowel.). Not *too* hard, was it? "King George was my favorite English ruler." Theoretically it could have been "King Greg" but our knowledge of British royalty makes it clear that "George" was intended.

It so happens that Hebrew developed early on a system of utilizing several weak consonants (especially H, W, and Y) to represent vowel sounds in certain instances. W = U, O; Y = I, E; and H = A, E, O were possible options (but with H used like this only at the end of a word). Under this arrangement the above sentence might have been spelled: KYNG GWRG WS MY FVWRYT *NGLYSH RWLR. Clearly an improvement, wouldn't you say? This would be especially welcome in more obscure contexts. For the reading of the Hebrew Old Testament these added symbols known as "vowel letters" can be extremely helpful. By the time of the writing of I and II Chronicles, such vowel letters were in substantial use.

One further point regarding the Hebrew alphabet: all Hebrew words begin with a consonant. That even includes names such as Abraham, Obadiah, and Uzziah! Hebrew has two consonants that are pretty much silent, the ALEPH (transcribed as ') and the AYIN (transcribed as '). Most Old Testament names that begin with a vowel in English begin with either ALEPH (as with Abraham) or AYIN (as with Obadiah and Uzziah). The consonant itself does not tell you what the following vowel should be. This must be learned from other means. Representing Hebrew in English (or "Roman") transcription, the name Abraham is spelled 'BRHM. Obadiah is 'BDYH. Hebrew does not write doubled letters, so the name Uzziah would simply be spelled 'ZYH.

Centuries after the time of Christ a new feature was added to the spelling of Hebrew. Various systems of vowel markings gradually developed. These consisted of sequences of dots and dashes that were added above, below, inside of and next to the original consonants. With these markings, known as "vowel pointing," the full complement of long and short vowels could be represented, as could other features such as the doubling of letters (indicated by a dot inside the letter). Eventually a full system of accentuation was added. The Hebrew Bible that most use today was produced by Jewish scribes from Tiberias in Galilee. They are called the Masoretes, coming from the word meaning "tradition," since they were responsible for the precise transmission of the text, both written and pronounced. The Hebrew Bible produced by them is known as the Masoretic Text. The time of the flourishing of Masoretic activity was approximately A.D. 500-900. The particular manuscript generally employed as THE Masoretic Text, known as the Leningrad Codex (preserved in St. Petersburg —formerly Leningrad— in Russia) dates from around A.D. 1000.

Let's conclude our brief overview by showing a few samples of what Hebrew looks like. We will use our I Chronicles 4:9-10 passage to display several forms.

Word	Transcription	Unpointed Form	Pointed Form
"Jabez"	YA'BETS	יעבץ	יַעְבֵּץ
"You would bless me"	TeBARaKÉNI*	תברכני	תְּבָרֲכֵנִי
"from harm"	MERA'AH	מרעה	מֵרָעָה

* Vowels not capitalized represent very short or "half" vowels. Unless a stress sign so indicates, Hebrew words are accented on the last syllable. The transcriptions offered in this book do not precisely follow the modern technical conventions for reading Hebrew. The Hebrew vowel "A" is pronounced *ah* as in "father." The "E" is pronounced as in "they."

THE DISCOVERY THAT CHANGES *EVERYTHING*

We are now ready to break some really new ground regarding our understanding of the prayer of Jabez. The results will surprise you. They did me! As we attempt to proceed, let's review the situation so far.

We have seen that the prayer of Jabez is probably *not* tied to some emotional trauma he wrestled with because of his humiliating name, as some have alleged. The name "Jabez" sounded similar to the word for pain, but his mother transposed the last two consonants so that his name would not be the humiliating "Jazeb," that is, "He's a pain." His name was likely *not* a weight dragging him down and driving him to throw himself upon God's mercy as has been imagined.

We have also noted that the concluding words of Jabez's prayer express a desire to be kept from pain or distress, not a loftier goal to spare others from the same.

Of the numerous English translations and paraphrases now out there, the New King James Version is the only one that renders the Hebrew expression as "that I may not cause pain." A noble thought is thus presented, but one that is almost certainly not in the original expression. Nevertheless Jabez promoters have chosen to rely on this reading to bolster their approach to the prayer. *This reading is misleading and should be rejected.*

Jabez prayed for more land, not more spiritual influence or greater opportunities to serve God. While the expression "enlarge my territory" may now today be serving as a stirring metaphor for our desire to be used by God, for Jabez it simply meant "give me more land." For Jabez, this gift would be a sign of God's blessing upon him, and his request no doubt arose from a real need or distress ("pain") in his life. We do not know how God worked out the acquisition of more land by Jabez, whether through conflict or negotiation or other means, but no doubt the acquisition involved additional "good land," pasturage for Jabez's herds.

We have raised the question whether or not Jabez's prayer might have a more poetic quality than our current understanding would suggest. Many prayers in the Old Testament utilize Hebrew parallelism, the balancing of thoughts in consecutive lines. This one feature most characterizes Hebrew writing as poetry. As we will now argue, Jabez's prayer may contain this poetic balancing in a greater way than previously recognized, rather than resemble a broader, more random "wish-list."

The most telling issue of all, however, is that *the Hebrew text as it is generally understood simply does not make good sense*. Translators and commentators have wrestled with the expression "do (make) from harm" without much success. Their decision has been basically to ignore the problem and provide what is demanded by context, or at least what would *seem* to be demanded by context. And so they render the Hebrew verb 'ASAH as something like "keep" or "deliver" or the like. This makes the problem go away. Or does it just hide the true solution? DETERMINING HOW THIS HEBREW VERB CAN MEAN JUST WHAT IT OUGHT TO MEAN IS THE KEY TO UNDERSTANDING CORRECTLY THE PRAYER OF JABEZ. **Let's now solve the puzzle. . . .**

We noted earlier that the Hebrew language used in writing the Old Testament was written primarily without vowel indicators. It was only centuries later, long after the time of Christ, that the Jewish scribes known as the Masoretes provided vowel pointings to indicate how *they* believed the words in the ancient text should be vocalized. The Masoretes, however, were not infallible. Mistakes of varying kinds occurred as they carried out their work. In one sense, their accuracy and reliability is truly amazing. And yet on occasion they failed to properly understand the correct situation behind a particular word (the Hebrew Old Testament has over 300,000 words!). At times the earlier Septuagint (Greek) translators had a better handle on the meaning of a term, although the overall results of their efforts were mixed. Occasionally the scholars who have produced our modern English translations have also departed from the Masoretes' vowel pointings to give us alternative meanings.

WHAT IF the Masoretic vowels supplied for a key word in Jabez's prayer were wrong? This would be no challenge to the accuracy of the original text of Scripture, since the originally written consonants would still be preserved. But a challenge it *would* be to the popular Jabez Movement! Why? Because the change I am proposing would change EVERYTHING!

The word that requires renewed scrutiny actually is not the word 'ASITA (from 'ASAH, "do, make,"), but rather the following word, MERA'AH, which is universally translated as "from harm" or "from evil." However, *the Hebrew letters MR'H also could be vocalized as MIR'EH*, a word that occurs elsewhere (thirteen times) in the Old Testament. In fact, IT OCCURS THREE TIMES AT THE END OF THIS VERY CHAPTER, AT I CHRONICLES 4:39, 40, 41! And guess what it means. . .Would you believe **PASTURE**

LAND! *The very thing Jabez most certainly desired in his request for God to enlarge his territory.*

We also need to remember that 'ASAH can carry the idea of "provide" as well as to "make" or "do" (the New International Version so renders it as "provide" some twenty times). David's rebellious son Absalom did not "make" ('ASAH) for himself a chariot and fifty runners to serve as a royal entourage, rather he "provided" them for himself (II Samuel 15:1). The Israelites did not wonder how they could "make" wives for the diminished Benjamite tribe, but how they could "provide" ('ASAH) them, since they had sworn not to give their own daughters to them in marriage (Judges 21:7, 16). *This meaning fits perfectly with our passage about Jabez.*

Jabez asked God to bless him by providing what he needed. He wanted God to *enlarge his territory* and he wanted God's "hand" to be upon him. In doing so (note the closer *parallelism* here now with the previous words), he wanted God to *provide him pasture land* so that he would no longer be in distress or duress ('ATSAB). So he prayed, **"Enlarge my territory . . . and PROVIDE ME WITH PASTURE LAND . . . ."** This rendering fits the context of the concern for pasture land in I Chronicles. This also produces a literary structure exhibiting poetic parallelism. *This, I'm* *convinced, **was** the **original** prayer of Jabez,* what I call "The *Lost* Prayer of Jabez"!

But how could the Jewish Masoretes and all translators of this passage up until now have MISSED WHAT SEEMS SO OBVIOUS? I think the answer must lie in the last word of the prayer, 'OTSBI, "cause me 'pain'" (a Hebrew infinitive form). The association between that Hebrew root and the other root from which we get the word "harm" or "evil" (RA'AH) was too suggestive to enable interpreters to step back and reassess the whole picture. The two roots naturally seem to go together—disaster and distress. So much so that the likelihood has not been recognized that we are dealing with *another* RA'AH root in Hebrew, one which means to "feed" or "shepherd" animals. The root denoting "disaster, harm, evil" occurs over 300 times; the root meaning "feed, shepherd, pasture" over 170 times. Context and grammar dictate which root is involved in a given instance.

What seems clear now is that the use of "pain" or "distress" at the end of the passage describes the condition that will ensue if Jabez's herds are not provided with more pasturage. Is this a fair meaning to attach to the term in such a context? Definitely, as a quick survey will show.

We are dealing here with a Biblical Hebrew root involving a verb, 'ATSAB, "to cause grief, distress,

---

The Two-fold Curse

An interesting connection now unfolds regarding this account and that of the Fall in Genesis 3. Each involve the use of the root 'ATSAB in connection with both childbirth ("pain"; Genesis 3:16, that which was experienced by Jabez's mother) and working the land ("toil"; Genesis 3:17, that which Jabez wanted a measure of relief from). The term for both the "pain" of childbirth and the "toil" associated with working the land there in Genesis 3 is the derivative form 'ITSABON. This connection makes it even more likely that Jabez's prayer focuses on the acquisition of productive land. His mother suffered with the "distress" allotted to women; he asks for relief from the "distress" allotted to men.

My thanks to Dr. John Walton at Wheaton College for this insight and others as we were discussing my book.

---

pain," and two nouns signifying "pain, distress," 'ETSEB (six times) and 'OTSEB (three times). 'OTSEB and 'ETSEB would appear to be interchangeable, and in fact would look identical in the original form of the Hebrew spelling before the Masoretes added their vowel pointing. In the vast majority of cases, physical pain is *not* what is involved, rather grief or distress. Let's note how our root is used. Noun or verb, the range of meaning is the same. Words in caps reflect this root's rendering in the New International Version. When God saw man's wickedness before the flood He was

GRIEVED (Genesis 6:6). David's lack of discipline regarding his son Adonijah is described by the Bible's saying that he had never INTERFERED WITH him (I Kings 1:6). The Babylonian captivity is described as trouble and SORROW (Isaiah 14:3). Psalm 127:2 speaks of those who TOIL for the bread they eat (See also Proverbs 5:10; 10:22 for the meaning "toil."). Proverbs 14:23 claims there is profit in HARD WORK. "Hard work," "toil," "distress," "sorrow"—all these can be conveyed by the "pain" word in our text.

It is easy to see, then, how the root 'ATSAB would naturally fit the context of Jabez's prayer. The lack of ample space and sufficient lush grazing land would definitely create a situation of being "pained." As a poetic device, the use of 'ATSAB closes a passage that has already introduced the connection between Jabez's name and the concept of 'OTSEB, "pain, distress." *However, ironically, this important stylistic feature of the prayer served to camouflage the real content of that prayer from future generations.*

Until now. What a fascinating verse!

Further Note: Several who reviewed earlier stages of this work suggested I provide another example of where the vowel pointing could be called into question. There are several, but here's a classic example.

In Isaiah 49:17 we find the word BNYK, vocalized by the Masoretes as BANAYIK, "your sons," in the passage "your sons hasten, your devastators and destroyers depart from you." The same letters,

however, could theoretically be read as BONAYIK, "your builders."
Generally the context would make the choice quite clear. Here, though,
we find a context in which either makes sense. The reference to the city's
walls at verse 16 would favor "builders," but the later reference to
"children" (the same Hebrew word that is translated "sons" in verse 17)
at verse 20 could be used to argue for "sons" at verse 17. Which reading
should it be?

Well, our translations can't agree on this one. The King James,
New King James, and New International Versions each prefer "sons,"
thus following the Masoretic pronunciation. On the other hand, the
New American Standard, Revised Standard, New Revised Standard,
New English Bible and most other recent translations opt for the reading
"builders." Part of their reason for doing so is that both the Greek Old
Testament (the "Septuagint," LXX) and the Dead Sea Scrolls (The
Great Isaiah Scroll, designated IQIsaᵃ) show the reading "builders."
Again, either reading fits the context. I don't mean to answer a question
with a question, but this case at Isaiah 49:17, I think, is a good example
of the issues involved with certain words in the Hebrew Old Testament
text.

Speaking to this whole issue again, we find in the preface to the
Revised Standard Version (Second Edition, 1971) the following
explanation:

The present revision is based on the consonantal Hebrew
and Aramaic text as fixed in the Christian era and revised by Jewish
scholars (the "Masoretes") of the sixth to ninth centuries. The vowel
signs, which were added by the Masoretes, are accepted also in the
main, but *where a more probable and convincing reading can be obtained*
by assuming different vowels, this has been done [italics mine]. No
notes are given in such cases, because the vowel points are less
ancient and reliable than the consonants.

I am convinced that at I Chronicles 4:10, the "Prayer of Jabez,"
I have provided a "more probable and convincing reading."

Larry Pechawer

The KEY to the *Lost* Prayer of Jabez

The unpointed form in standard "block letters":

The alternate "pointed" forms:

MERA'AH
"From Evil"

MIR'EH
"Pasture Land"

THE LOST PRAYER OF JABEZ

Now Jabez cried out to the God of Israel saying,

If You would only bless me,

then **enlarge my territory**
  that Your hand may be with me,

and **provide me with pasture land**
  so that I will not be in distress.

And God brought about that which he had requested.

I Chronicles 4:10

Summary of the arguments to this point.

ARE YOU *SURE* IT SAYS "PASTURE LAND"?

Most people who see or hear my re-translation for the first time get a puzzled look on their faces. It is quite an adjustment, isn't it? At this point, then, I think it would be helpful to summarize the arguments in favor of this new understanding. Although absolute certainty perhaps cannot be achieved, there are many good reasons to take this new read on the passage. Here's a list of reasons for your consideration.

Reason #1

The fact that Jabez's prayer has had a "checkered" past supports our reading of "pasture land." As the final chapter will illustrate in detail, "The Prayer of Jabez" has plagued translators and interpreters from the beginning. The mistaken reading of the ancient Septuagint (LXX) has already been noted. The awkward combination of the words "MAKE, PROVIDE" ('ASAH) and "FROM EVIL" (MERA'AH) did not suggest itself to those early Jewish scholars. Instead, they read the Hebrew letter "R" as a "D" (letters almost identical in appearance) and came up with MADDA'AH, an unusual form of the Hebrew word "KNOWLEDGE." Therefore in their Greek translation (rendering the key word above as GNŌSIS, "knowledge"), the meaning was something like, "Make me *know* that You will not cause me pain." (!)

Later Jewish and Christian translators fared no better. The Jewish translation into Aramaic was known as the "targum" (meaning "translation"). It shows a very fanciful rendering of Jabez's prayer, as we will later see. Aramaic was the language that Jesus spoke and was the language utilized by the Jews even more than Hebrew following their return from the Babylonian captivity.

Eastern Christians also spoke a dialect of Aramaic often referred to as "Syriac." In the Syriac Bible (called the "Peshitta"), a very important ancient witness to the text of Scripture, we again find a fanciful, confused rendering of this prayer. But in no way does it resemble the Jewish Targum of Chronicles. Jews and Christians went their separate ways on this text, with both going far afield from what it originally said. Neither ancient tradition is close to what we find in our English Bibles.

More will be said in the final chapter, but suffice it here to say that the sense and significance of Jabez's prayer has not been agreed upon by interpreters, ancient or modern. What's missing here? I think that I have provided the answer.

Reason #2

The fact that the combination 'ASAH + MERA'AH does not make good sense supports the reading "pasture land." The strongest "proof" that my translation is correct is that *the Hebrew text as it has been generally understood simply does not make good sense.* Translators and commentators have wrestled with the expression "do (make) from harm" without much success. Their decision has been basically to ignore the problem and provide what is demanded by context, or at least what would *seem* to be demanded by context. In doing so, they have missed the true solution.

The Hebrew verb 'ASAH occurs *over 2,600 times* in the Old Testament, and NEVER with the sense proposed by our English translations here in the Prayer of Jabez.

We have shown that 'ASAH can carry the idea of "provide" as well as to "make" or "do" (the New International Version so renders it as "provide" some twenty times). David's rebellious son Absalom "provided" ('ASAH) a royal entourage for himself

(II Samuel 15:1). The Israelites wondered how they could "provide" ('ASAH) wives for the diminished Benjamite tribe, since they had sworn not to give their own daughters to them in marriage (Judges 21:7, 16). *This meaning fits perfectly with our passage.*

We also noted that the association between the Hebrew root for "pain, distress," and the root meaning "harm" or "evil" (RA'AH, from a root R'') was so close that it prevented interpreters from recognizing that we are dealing with *another* RA'AH root in Hebrew, one which means to "feed" or "shepherd" animals. The root denoting "disaster, harm, evil" occurs over 300 times; the one meaning "feed, shepherd, pasture" over 170 times. The context and grammar involved in Jabez's prayer make it very likely that the latter root is involved here.

Reason #3

The immediate context of the passage supports the reading "pasture land." As noted in the last chapter, the Jewish Masoretes pronounced the key word in question as MERA'AH, which is universally translated as "from harm" or "from evil." However, *the Hebrew letters MR'H also could be vocalized as MIR'EH,* a word that occurs elsewhere (thirteen times) in the Old Testament. In fact, IT OCCURS THREE TIMES AT THE END OF THIS VERY CHAPTER, AT I

CHRONICLES 4:39, 40, 41! And it means **PASTURE LAND**! *The was something Jabez certainly desired in his request for God to enlarge his territory.*

For the sake of completeness, here are the other instances of MIR'EH, "pasture land," that are found in the Hebrew Old Testament: Genesis 47:4; Isaiah 32:14, 40; Ezekiel 34:14 (twice), 18 (twice); Joel 1:18; Lamentations 1:6; Job 39:8; and Nahum 2:12 (some prefer to read M'RH, "cave," here). A related word from the same RA'AH root, MAR'IT, can also have the meaning of "pasturage." See Isaiah 49:9 and Jeremiah 25:36.

It seems pretty obvious that the request for expanded territory and quality grazing land for herds go together. Am I missing something here?

Reason #4

The overall context of I&II Chronicles supports the reading "pasture land." Many of the genealogical records in I Chronicles are tied to various tribal land possessions in the Promised Land. Also, elsewhere in the Old Testament there is an emphasis on grazing land for the herds of the Levites who lived in the forty-eight Levitical cities. We learn that "Each of these towns had pasturelands surrounding it; this was true for all these towns" (Joshua 21:42). The dimensions specified in Numbers 35:1-5 for pasture land for the

Levitical cities involved a square surrounding each city measuring three thousand feet on each side. Praying for "pasture land" starts to make more sense when the setting is better understood.

We earlier noted the request of Achsah, daughter of the Judahite chieftain Caleb. "Give me a blessing!" it says in the original Hebrew (NIV translates "Do me a special favor.") Her father had given her land, but she wanted to make sure that adequate water resources were available. And so she requested, **"Do me a special favor. Since you have given me land in the Negev, give me also springs of water." So Caleb gave her the upper and lower springs (Joshua 15:19).** Land itself wasn't enough for Achsah. She wanted the right kind of land. So did Jabez.

We should also note that Chronicles shows a special interest in prayers uttered by leaders in distress. King Asa (II Chronicles 14), King Jehoshaphat (II Chronicles 20), and King Manasseh (II Chronicles 33) each offered prayers that God answered in a favorable manner. Jabez was a distinguished leader in Judah, not a king, but his request from God resulted in a blessing, just as the kings' requests did. For example, God's answer of Jehoshaphat's prayer resulted in the renaming of a valley where the people had gathered to bless the Lord. They called it the Valley of Berakah, the "Valley of Blessing" (II Chronicles 20:26).

Some might be concerned that my version of the Prayer of Jabez seems a bit "unspiritual." Well, let's keep reading a few verses down from Jabez's prayer and look at another petition that God answered. In I Chronicles 5:18-22 we read about a military conflict between the Israelite tribes of Reuben, Gad, and Manasseh on one hand, and the Hagrites and their allies on the other. The key verse is verse twenty:

They were helped in fighting them, and God handed the Hagrites and all their allies over to them, because they cried out to him during the battle. He answered their prayers, because they trusted in him.

The result? The Israelites seized the livestock of the Hagrites, took their land, took many captives and killed many others, because "the battle was God's" (I Chronicles 5:21-22). The Israelites entered into this campaign trusting God for the victory and He delivered them from their enemies. This account provides part of the broader context for the Prayer of Jabez—territory, livestock, servants, even bloodshed. Doesn't fit today's popular approach, does it?

Reason #5

The theological implications of the statement following the prayer favor the reading "pasture land." Not enough attention has been paid to the theological implications of the statement following Jabez's prayer– "And God brought about that which he had requested" (my translation). Exactly what's involved with that? Remember the last part of the alleged prayer? "Keep me from harm/evil." So did God do that? For the duration of Jabez's life on earth? Or was it a short-term arrangement, maybe a one-time deal? The text itself places no limits on the language. Do you see the problem? It's one thing for Jesus to teach us to pray "Deliver us from evil." It's quite another thing for someone (Jabez) to pray such a prayer and receive a life-long security contract! Frankly, there are serious problems with the way this prayer is currently understood. My alternative reading is linguistically, contextually, and, yes, theologically compelling.

Reason #6

A newly appreciated parallel construction within the prayer results from the reading "pasture land." As noted earlier, many prayers in Scripture contain poetic parallelism. Unlike the poetry of English and many other languages, Hebrew poetry does not generally rhyme. What Hebrew poetry does exhibit is *parallelism*, a balancing of terms or thoughts. This parallelism is the primary characteristic of Hebrew poetry. The recovered "Lost Prayer" would also seem to contain an element of "recovered" poetic parallelism. The components "Enlarge my territory" and "Provide me with pasture land" are parallel, along with the corresponding results—"that Your hand may be with me" and "so that I will not be in distress." This stylistic, literary argument is not conclusive, of course, but it does support the position being presented here.

Reason #7

A connection with the curses found in Genesis 3 now results from the reading "pasture land." An intriguing connection now unfolds regarding this account and that of the Fall in Genesis 3, as John Walton (Wheaton College) pointed out to me. Each account involves the use of the root 'ATSAB in connection with both childbirth ("pain"; Genesis 3:16, that which was experienced by Jabez's mother) and working the land ("toil"; Genesis 3:17, that which Jabez wanted a measure of relief from). The term for both the "pain" of childbirth and the "toil" associated with working the land there in Genesis 3 is the derivative form 'ITSABON. This connection makes it even more likely that Jabez's prayer focuses on the acquisition of productive land. His mother suffered from the "distress" allotted to women; he asks for relief from the "distress" allotted to men.

Reason #8

Evidence from antiquity that, indeed, other ancient people prayed for "pasture land" supports our reading. One of the most fascinating ancient inscriptions ever found is located on a stone statue of a Syrian (Aramaean) ruler named Had-yithi. Had-yithi was king of the city of Guzana (Biblical Gozan), in the Khabur-Balikh region north of the Euphrates River. He ruled during the latter half of the 9th century B.C. Discovered in 1979, the statue was found roughly two miles away at Tell Fakhariyah, the site of ancient Sikanu.

The inscription itself is actually found on the *skirt* that the figure of Had-yithi is depicted as wearing: Assyrian writing on the front, Aramaic on the back. The skirt of Had-yithi contains the first substantial bilingual Aramaic-Assyrian text ever discovered. This inscription contains many suprising linguistic features that have been carefully analyzed by various scholars. I've looked at this text, especially the Aramaic portion, many times over the years, but a phrase at its beginning takes on a new significance in light of my re-interpretation of the Prayer of Jabez.

It may be asked whether or not the notion of "praying for pasture land" could actually represent a

meaningful prayer in antiquity. It's not a prayer we hear too often these days! Well, I can't point to a specific example of such a prayer in the ancient world. Perhaps the Assyriologists can come up with one for us among the many thousands of cuneiform inscriptions now known.

> *The Syrian god Hadad is referred to as "the provider of pasture and watering place" by his worshipers.*

But really we don't need one. *What we have is just as good.* The Tell Fakhariyah text clearly shows that the "gods" of ancient nations were called on by their devotees to provide good grazing land and abundant water sources. The patron god of Sikanu, Hadad, is addressed in the opening lines of this text with a series of epithets or titles describing Hadad as the benefactor of his people. He is described as the "irrigation master of heaven and earth" and the one "who makes all lands luxuriant." (These descriptions of this particular god are commonly found

> *The great king Hammurabi called himself "the provider of pasture land and watering places."*

elsewhere as well.) In lines two and three of the Aramaic text (Assyrian line two) the Syrian god Hadad is referred

71

to as "the provider of pasture and watering place" (following the translation of Dr. Stephen A. Kaufman in his "Reflections on the Assyrian-Aramaic Bilingual from Tell Fakhariyeh," in the journal *MAARAV* 3/2 [1982]:137-175). Since ancient deities were often described in terms of what their worshipers viewed as important, it's logical that Hadad's followers actually sought what he is described as having provided: pasture land and watering places!

In support of this proposal we can also point to one of the most famous rulers of antiquity—Hammurabi, King of Babylon. A king who lived well before the time of Jabez, Hammurabi chose to refer to himself in terms of what his subjects greatly desired, and thus called himself "the provider of pasture land and watering places." (See, e.g., W. W. Hallo and K. L. Younger, *The Context of Scripture, Vol. II: Monumental Inscriptions from the Biblical World*, Brill 2000, pp. 257, 336.)

So both gods and kings of antiquity are spoken of in glowing terms as "providers of pasture land."

(NOTE: In the Aramaic text at Tell Fakhariyah, the word RE'I, "pasture land," is a different noun construction from MIR'EH, but is based on the same root, RA'AH, meaning "shepherd, pasture.")

Reason #9

A greater appreciation of Jabez's prayer as an ancient, authentic prayer results from the reading "pasture land." Okay, maybe this is more of a result than a reason, but I think it is a significant point for Bible believers. Chronicles has not fared well at the hands of some Old Testament critics. It has been viewed as secondary, legendary, unreliable and basically unhistorical. It paints a more "religious" picture (spell that "untrustworthy") than Samuel or Kings, according to critics, and therefore should be used with caution. This is not the place to enter into that well-known, ongoing discussion. For our purposes, however, it would be well to point out the implications for this discussion from the various takes on Jabez's prayer.

The current understanding of the Jabez Movement fits in well (not intentionally) with the approach that prayers such as those put in the mouth of Jabez and other more prominent Old Testament figures are in conformity with the concerns of the later Jewish community and reflect the concerns of the post-exilic priesthood and leadership. It has been suggested that Jabez's prayer was inserted as a refreshing change from the sinful practices of many of the leaders chronicled in Scripture. Jabez's "super spirituality" fits well into the religiosity that permeates the later books of I&II Chronicles. Whether this spirituality was real or contrived by the author of Chronicles is what some Biblical scholars choose to debate.

But note what happens when my proposed translation is embraced. *Jabez's prayer for territory and pasture land can hardly be viewed as anything but an authentic ancient prayer that was recorded for future generations.* What other explanation would there be? Like other pray-ers in Chronicles, Jabez serves as an example of an honored, notable leader who trusted in God to provide his needs, and He did. The precise things prayed for are to some extent irrelevant. <u>We should follow Jabez's example of praying in faith, *not his example of what to pray for.*</u>

At any rate, it appears to me that the prayer for pasture land stems out of a real historical situation, not from a later theological agenda. It is true that the post-exilic Jewish community was interested in land, but it is hard for me to imagine that the request for "pasture land" was the product of a later writer of that day. In sum, my version of the Prayer of Jabez has the ring of antiquity and authenticity to it.

Reason #10

Without altering the original Hebrew text, a more convincing translation is provided with the reading "pasture land." As scholars and translators of Scripture have known all along, at times the later vowel pointing of the Jewish Masoretic scribes should be abandoned, so that the original inspired consonantal text can convey a more likely meaning. Again, we note the preface to the Revised Standard Version (Second Edition, 1971):

The present revision is based on the consonantal Hebrew and Aramaic text. . . . The vowel signs, which were added by the Masoretes, are accepted also in the main, but *where a more probable and convincing reading can be obtained by assuming different vowels, this has been done* [italics mine].

I believe that for the "Prayer of Jabez," I have provided, in the words of the RSV translators, a "more probable and convincing reading."

In view of the above arguments, it is my recommendation that future translations of the Bible incorporate at I Chronicles 4:10 what I have called "The Lost Prayer of Jabez."

SO I'M CONVINCED...
NOW WHAT?

Well now you have it. In spite of the efforts of various Jewish and Christian interpreters, I am convinced that there was a "Jabez we never knew." This Jabez wanted more *pasture land*, not freedom from sin, harm, temptation, or whatever. That's what the *original* prayer of Jabez says. Missing this key to the prayer has caused translators throughout the centuries to struggle with this text, always with unsatisfactory results. For corroboration and confirmation from other Hebrew scholars, teachers, and church leaders regarding my approach, see the next chapter.

Where does that leave us? "Expand my border... and provide me with pasture land...." This new understanding really does change *everything* with regard to any future discussion of this prayer, doesn't it? What Christian would pray *this* prayer in the context of worship and devotion to God? In light of this new information, however, some would now ask, "If I can't trust my Bible on *this* passage, how can I trust it on *any* passage?

Several observations need to be made. First, the reliability of our Bible in its present form should not be called into question. The Scriptures have been more carefully preserved throughout the centuries than any other writings from antiquity. Ancient Jewish traditions speak to the meticulous attention to detail in the work of copying their sacred records. However, the nature of the Hebrew does allow for some ambiguity in certain forms. Fortunately, the Greek New Testament Scriptures are written like English, with both consonants and vowels, and a greater level of certainty is realized. Any uncertainties existing in the Hebrew Old Testament do not measurably affect matters of doctrine, faith, or ethics. God's nature and will for his people come through loud and clear. His word is reliable.

Am I *certain* that my proposed new reading is what Jabez originally said? I've outlined in detail the arguments for my interpretaion. But no, I don't think absolute certainty can be achieved here. However, I think all roads point to my interpretation—Hebrew grammar, historical and literary context, the works. Even if absolute certainty can't be achieved, shouldn't the strong presumption of doubt now raised against the current understanding be a red flag for the "Jabez Movement"? Well, don't hold your breath. Millions have been invested to fuel the fires of this fad for as long as possible.

But even apart from the dramatically different interpretation presented here, does the Jabez phenomenon fairly represent what the Bible says in I Chronicles 4? Based on a host of concerns, many others are starting to question the whole idea of building so much upon such an obscure passage. There is no command stated in the text. As well, there is no hint that this serves as some precedent for others to follow. At best the passage is illustrative. It is true that the Old Testament serves to give us examples to follow (I Corinthians 10:11). Usually such examples are accompanied by divine statements of commendation or condemnation. We generally don't have to guess on the intended application.

The Jabez promoters are guilty of "retrofitting" an alleged application for us back into Jabez's own situation. Jabez is portrayed as asking God for more "influence," more "opportunity for service," more "ability" to be used by God. All of this is smuggled back into the text by overzealous expositors.

Back to the *actual* text: Jabez asked God for LAND. What I have tried to present here is the significance of the land in Jabez's *own* setting and to understand the passage in light of that. From that point on, *proceed with caution.*

To put the current situation in perspective I think it is only fair to reiterate that the Jabez promoters cannot be faulted for missing the interpretation I have presented. No available translations or resources present this. What they can be faulted for is an overly enthusiastic exploitation of this account. What God never said (*why* He favorably answered the prayer), the current promoters are filling in for us. And now the problem is compounded, if my view be accepted, because the passage doesn't say what we've generally assumed it says. The result is that the strongly spiritual dimension of the prayer is gone. The "original" Jabez may not quite have lived up to his current stellar billing.

One of the challenges that modern expositors have is to analyze Scriptural accounts and statements in light of their original context or setting. It should be noted that the prayer of Jabez is found in a portion of Scripture that emphasizes the prayers of God's people. And not only that, it is affirmed there that God answered such prayers.

In I and II Chronicles we often find a focus more directed toward the religious aspects of Israel's history than we find in the books of Samuel and Kings. The temple and its rituals, the priestly and Levitical functions, the Davidic dynasty, and personal piety and worship are elements we frequently encounter. On the other hand, we find no account of the events of the apostate Northern Kingdom paralleling those recorded in Kings, and only a single chapter concerning King Saul (I Chronicles 10—relating the circumstances of his death).

Sometimes the accounts in Chronicles contain prayers uttered by kings, prayers that are not reported in connection with those same kings in the records in I and II Kings. King Asa (II Chronicles 14), King Jehoshaphat (II Chronicles 20), and King Manasseh (II Chronicles 33) each offered prayers not recorded in Kings or elsewhere. In each case, God answered the prayer in a favorable manner. Jabez was no king (though an "honored" leader), but his request for a blessing from God resulted in a blessing bestowed, as it was with the above-mentioned kings.

Each of those kings also prayed in a time of distress. Each received deliverance, a "blessing." As noted, God's answer of Jehoshaphat's prayer resulted in the renaming of a valley where the people had gathered to bless the Lord. They called it the Valley of Berakah, the "Valley of Blessing" (II Chronicles 20:26).

For Jabez, deliverance from "distress" involved the blessing of new, productive land. The record of His petition and God's response is paralleled by other accounts in I and II Chronicles. Jabez stands in a tradition of pray-ers in these books.

My proposed rereading of Jabez's prayer may prompt other related questions. What about all the answered prayers in connection with the current Jabez phenomenon? According to umpteen testimonies, "Praying Jabez" really works! Well, maybe we should say *praying* really works. One of the bright spots of this whole matter is the emphasis on seeking God's involvement in our lives. But seeking God's blessing is not the private property of Jabez in Scripture. Nor is the example of answered prayer. And if the truth be known, sometimes "Praying Jabez" *hasn't* worked out so well.

Some of the thoughts expressed in "Jabez prayers" are things found elsewhere in Scripture. They are legitimate topics of prayer. This present work, however, brings into serious doubt whether such sentiments can be derived from Jabez's prayer. Jesus offered us a model prayer in which we are to ask for deliverance from evil or the "evil one" (Matthew 6:13). Jabez's prayer likely contained no such request. The Apostle Paul prayed that God would provide him greater avenues of service and the ability to influence others for God in a mighty way (Colossians 4:2-6). Jabez prayed no such prayer, if our understanding of the text is correct.

An important question arises from this study, but one that lies outside its narrow scope. If Jabez's prayer was basically a request for material blessings, how does that apply to Christians today living under the New Covenant? I mention the New Covenant because the Hebrew Scriptures show that *Old* Covenant Israel was promised material blessing as a result of their faithfulness to God. I do not find such a material prosperity connection for believers under the New Covenant. The patriarchs Abraham, Isaac, and Jacob were wealthy. The twelve apostles were not. The curses of the Old Covenant included the failure of the land to yield its crops and, eventually, the removal of God's people from that land (Leviticus 26; Deuteronomy 28). The New Testament reveals a judgment of God that relates primarily to life after death.

Again, this is not the place to develop a theology of wealth or prosperity. It only makes sense, however, that the prayer of Jabez should be relegated to its proper place—a prayer for the kind of blessing that God promised those who lived under the old dispensation of law, one tied directly to the fortunes of national Israel and its land. On the other hand, the New Testament's warnings about the love of money and the preoccupation with "more" (as in Jesus's mention of "bigger and bigger barns") are well known. Whatever our economic lot, it is essential that we are "rich toward God" (Luke 12:21). In this regard, I think the warning uttered by Carl F. H. Henry is helpful:

The temptation that we can best serve God, or neighbor, through the amassing of wealth, or power, or the prestige of some human office, is a dangerous one. He best serves God and man who loves them above all else, and does not make his affection for them a reflex of a deeper love for money, glory, or whatever else. When love for God is second, it is not love for God at all. An idol then stands

83

at the center of life, and all other motivations, love of man included, are endangered (*Christian Personal Ethics*, Baker 1977, p. 395).

Let me say that I do not read the "health and wealth gospel" *per se* in Bruce Wilkinson's words. There is, however, an all too easy transition toward that idea from a prayer motif that emphasizes a self-oriented approach regarding God's blessings. "Bless me and my . . ." is the recurring theme promoted by the Jabez Movement, a theme built upon Jabez's supposed words in I Chronicles 4:10. It is a theme that certainly resonates with the current culture confronting the Church of the Living God.

A theology of prayer must depend upon a broad Biblical overview. As others have reminded, there are many great prayers in the Bible to study and emulate. In addition to those of our Lord, we can note the prayers of Moses (Numbers 14), David (various Psalms, e. g., Psalm 51), Solomon (I Kings 8), Hezekiah (Isaiah 37), Hannah (I Samuel 1), Mary (Luke 1), and Nehemiah 9, to name a few. The translation and interpretation of these prayers are clear. Meaningful application to our own lives is abundant as we mine the riches found within these and other great texts.

I don't think we will ever outlive the increased usage of the metaphor **"enlarge my territory!"** It is a landmark now on the contemporary Christian scene. But I hope that in the not too distant future we will see it become less of a formulaic summons and more of a simple figure of speech.

As Christians seeking God's power in our lives, how could we find a better model than Paul's marvelous prayer at Ephesians 3:14-21?

For this reason I kneel before the Father, from whom his whole family in heaven and on earth derives its name. I pray that out of his glorious riches he may strengthen you with power through his Spirit in your inner being, so that Christ may dwell in your hearts through faith. And I pray that you, being rooted and established in love, may have power, together with all the saints, to grasp how wide and long and high and deep is the love of Christ, and to know this love that surpasses knowledge–that you may be filled to the measure of all the fulness of God. Now to him who is able to do immeasurably more than all we ask or imagine, according to his power that is at work within us, to him be glory in the church and in Christ Jesus throughout all generations, for ever and ever! Amen.

Strengthened by the power of God's Spirit . . . established in love . . . filled with God's fulness . . . enabled beyond our imagination to ask or dream—all results of prayer to the One who specializes in the impossible. The *prayer* of Jabez in the final analysis may not be all that some have imagined it to be. But the *God* of Jabez will never disappoint.

(The following endorsements were offered by individuals who had received advance copies of the first edition.)

SCHOLARS AND LEADERS ENDORSING THESE FINDINGS

The author has provided a service for the Church both on the technical level by proposing a convincing retranslation of this difficult text, and on the practical level by alerting us to the potential abuse of the biblical text that could lead us to inappropriate conclusions about how we should approach God and what we should expect from Him.

DR. JOHN H. WALTON, *Professor of Old Testament, Wheaton College, Wheaton, IL.*

Larry Pechawer is the 'Grinch' that stole the 'Christmas of Jabez.' For many who have jumped on the wagon of the 'Prayer of Jabez' this small book is a necessary corrective to an unfortunate 'Jabez' fascination with some unfortunate biblical interpretations. I heartily agree with and endorse the author's 'Bah Humbug' as well as his enlightening new interpretation.

DR. WALTER D. ZORN, *Professor of Old Testament, Lincoln Christian College, Lincoln, IL.*

Thinking Christians, informed lay persons and pastors, I believe, will definitely benefit.

DR. STEPHEN M. HOOKS, Professor of Old Testament and Hebrew, Atlanta Christian College.

Larry, I think you are on to something. Your proposal makes a great deal of sense and helps the text fit better into the context of 1 Chronicles 4. It makes more sense from the cultural and sociological setting as well. Your work impresses me as a bold plea for sound exegesis and proper application of proper hermeneutical principles.

DR. GARY HALL, Professor of Old Testament and Hebrew, Lincoln Christian Seminary, Lincoln, IL.

In *The Lost Prayer of Jabez*, Larry Pechawer gets out his Hebrew tools, digs into the original text and comes up with some surprising, even stunning, results. Could Jabez have actually prayed for something other than what our standard English Bible translations have suggested? Discover for yourself the missing key to understanding the *original* prayer of Jabez.

VICTOR KNOWLES, Editor of One Body, *Director of Peace on Earth Ministries, Joplin, MO.*

As someone who was blessed by reading Bruce Wilkinson's The Prayer of Jabez, I was interested in finding what else there was to say about the topic. What I found in Larry Pechawer's book was much of the information that I wish I had heard from the beginning of my study of this prayer. No Bible study of this prayer is complete without reading what his research contributes to the discussion.

DAVID B. FINCHER, Academic Dean, Central Christian College of the Bible, Moberly, MO.

Fads, by default, are popular but not permanent. The word of God, however, is eternal. Larry Pechawer has done the church a valuable service here in distinguishing between the two. While great good has come from the "Prayer of Jabez" phenomenon, this little book in your hand relentlessly presses the more important issue: But what does the Bible actually say? If Pechawer is correct (and I'm convinced he is), then we're obligated to return to the other model prayers in the N.T. such as Paul's great prayer's in the epistles or perhaps even the prayer of Jesus, rather than Jabez.

MARK E. MOORE, Professor of New Testament, Ozark Christian College, Joplin, MO

Professor Pechawer has produced solid evidence that the popular interpretation of the prayer of Jabez in 1 Chronicles 4 does not represent sound translation or exegesis. His work compelled me to check the Hebrew for the verses involved, and Pechawer's comments are absolutely correct.

LLOYD M. PELFREY, Chancellor and Professor of Old Testament and Hebrew, Central Christian College of the Bible, Moberly, MO.

The Lost Prayer of Jabez makes me think of a statement from Warren and David Wiersbe. They said, 'A clever outline ruined by good exegesis' (The Elements of Preaching, 32). My co-worker, Larry Pechawer, has done his homework—and some won't like the results. But should a text mean what it never meant? Preachers have an obligation to declare the truth regardless of what pop theology is sweeping the land.

MARK SCOTT, Academic Dean, Ozark Christian Col-lege, Joplin, MO.

Mr. Pechawer's exposition of the prayer of Jabez is a two-fold success. Not only is his revelation convincing, but it is comprehendible by non-Hebrew scholars interested in sound Biblical interpretation.

TROY L. KINAST, High School Math and Bible School Teacher, Joplin, MO.

Larry Pechawer reminds us of the danger in applying a text spiritually before we know what it means. His careful analysis should not stop us from praying but should keep us from basing too much on too little.

DR. CARL BRIDGES, Professor of Bible, Johnson Bible College, Knoxville , TN.

MORE ABOUT JABEZ . . .

I hope you have enjoyed *The Lost Prayer of Jabez* so far. We've come to a point where some of you may want to sign off. For those who wish to dig deeper, I now provide further research on the history of Jabez's prayer through the centuries. This includes what I think are fascinating findings of how the ancient Jewish Sages and early Eastern Syrian Christians viewed Jabez and his prayer. This material is totally new to the evangelical Christian community. I am pleased to make this information available to you.

* **The Prayer of Jabez Through the Ages**

* **"Rabbi Jabez" and the Jewish Sages**

* **A Final Word for Specialists**

The Prayer of Jabez Through the Ages

The purpose of this section is to demonstrate what a wild ride this prayer has had throughout history. Translators have always wrestled with this prayer, sometimes with surprising results. It is my contention that the true content of this prayer has been "lost" for all these centuries, and, as a result, the attempts to force the original language of the prayer into some other meaning has created translations that have been unsatisfactory. Just think of all the current wrangling and debate on the proper application of the text. If you accept my translation of the Prayer of Jabez, the proper application (or lack thereof!) becomes pretty clear, doesn't it?

As we wend our way through the ancient attempts to render this passage, some of what will be presented will seem almost bizarre. Therefore, a bit of needed background explanation will accompany the more unique ancient translations. Enjoy the tour.

1. The Original Hebrew Consonantal Text

As we begin our journey, let's recall what has been said about the original text of the Old Testament. Written without special symbols for vowel sounds, ancient Hebrew was basically represented with consonants only. A system of using certain consonants for double duty—as indicators for both consonantal and vowel sounds—was developed during the thousand years leading up to the time of Christ. The letters H, W, and Y especially served to represent various vowels at times.

What turns out to be the key phrase in Jabez's prayer, We'ASITA MIR'EH, "and provide pasture land," was spelled W'SYT MR'H. This phrase actually contains two such vowel letters, the "Y" of the first word pronounced as the vowel "I," and the final "H" of MR'H pronounced as "E."

Other vowels in these two words must be determined from grammar and context. The Masoretes centuries after Christ developed the system of vowel markings we now find in the Hebrew manuscripts used as the basis of our printed Hebrew Bibles. Their efforts were enlightened but not inspired. Their results may have been "Ivory Soap" (remember the old "99 44/100ths %"?) pure, but they didn't always get it right. With some 300,000 words in the Hebrew Bible, let's not be surprised that some uncertainties existed and still do.

2. The Dead Sea Scrolls

The manuscripts found at and around the Dead Sea community of Qumran, texts more commonly referred to as the Dead Sea Scrolls, are of no help for our investigation of the Prayer of Jabez. There are two reasons. First, the Scrolls have preserved only a tiny fraction of the text of Chronicles: a brief section that overlaps the end of I Chronicles and the beginning of II Chronicles. Second, even if we had Jabez's prayer preserved in these documents, we would learn nothing new. The spelling of the critical words would be the same: W'SYT MR'H. (Possibly we would find an additional "H" to represent the final vowel "A" of the first word We'ASITA, but that form is not in doubt.) No further information would be gained from the Dead Sea Scrolls as to the pronunciation of those words or really of any of the words in the prayer.

3. The Greek "Septuagint" Translation c. 250 B. C. (done by Jews in Egypt)

The Septuagint is the earliest known translation of the Old Testament. Produced several centuries before Christ, the Septuagint reveals an alternate understanding of the text. The expression "make from evil" did not impress those early translators as the best way to go. They developed an entirely different approach.

At the time the book of Chronicles was written, the two letters "R" and "D" were virtually identical. Context is really the only sure guide in many cases.

Here, instead of reading MR'H (MERA'AH, "from harm"), the LXX translators read MD'H, which they took to signify MADDA'AH, meaning "knowledge" (an unusual spelling for the word usually given as simply MADDA'). They read this something like "and make me know (literally "make knowledge") that I will not suffer pain." Their rendering has attracted little if any following. The point here is simply that the LXX did not see 'ASITA MERA'AH, "make from evil," as a natural take ('ASITA is a form of 'ASAH). They were correct, I believe, in rejecting the term MR'H as being related to the word meaning "harm, evil," but their alternative was itself unsatisfactory.

The key Septuagint line of Jabez's prayer reads:

KAI   POIĒSĒS   GNŌSIN   TOU   MĒ TAPEINŌSAI   ME

Translating this is a struggle. Some suggest,

"And make (me) know (lit. "knowledge," GNŌSIN) that (You) will not humiliate me."

On the other hand, a more natural rendering of the Greek would be,

"And provide me with knowledge so that
I will not be humiliated" (lit. "so as not
to humiliate me").

This alternate translation would suggest that Jabez desired the gift of knowledge—a gift that would help him avoid being humbled or humiliated. Land and knowledge—not a very natural pair, is it?

The Septuagint of Chronicles was likely produced within several hundred years of the original writing of Chronicles. In light of these earlier translators' efforts, it would seem that, within a very short time, the original meaning of Jabez's prayer had already been "lost."

4. The Latin Vulgate c. A. D. 400.

Ironically, the first precisely datable evidence of the traditional understanding of the Prayer of Jabez comes from *Latin*, not Hebrew. The Old Testament of the Latin Vulgate was translated by Jerome in A. D. 390-405. It is true that there is an earlier Latin translation of the Bible generally referred to as the Old Latin. This is less readily available for study and is represented by various fragments and partial manuscripts scattered all over the world. It is also found in some quotations from various Church Fathers. (See Ernst Würthwein, *The Text of the Old Testament: An Introduction to the Biblica Hebraica* [Translated by Erroll F. Rhodes], Eerdmans, 1979.)

The study of Old Latin manuscripts is a highly specialized field. I invite any students of the Old Latin

Old Testament to investigate the reading of Jabez's prayer in that translation, if it can be found at all in existing sources. Since the Old Latin was based primarily on the Greek Septuagint, one could expect to find the same reading as that of the Septuagint (LXX), therefore, "And make me know that you will not humiliate me," or some such rendering. However, the Book of Chronicles has proved surprising at the hands of other ancient translators, so it cannot be automatically assumed how the Old Latin would have read.

Unlike the Old Latin, however, the Latin Vulgate was based on the Hebrew text. It reads:

ET FECERIS ME A MALITIA NON OPPRIMI

A rough translation would be something like: "And make me not be overcome by evil." This seems like a game attempt to translate an awkward Hebrew line. The Vulgate sounds a lot like the modern understanding of the prayer. That suggests that the understanding preserved in the later vowel points of the 6th-9th-century Masoretic scribes was already present in the 4th century A. D. As will be shown in the next section, there is other evidence to support the notion that this (wrong) interpretation was followed by the various Jewish sages through the years.

5. The Hebrew Masoretic Text (A.D. 900-1000)

The vowel "pointings" or markers supplied in the Masoretic Bible show a picture similar to the rendering in the Latin Vulgate. From these pointings we get the pronunciation MERA'AH, "from evil/harm," the reading that, in my view, has fostered an incorrect interpretation of the focus of Jabez's prayer in all subsequent foreign translations.

In a sense, by adding their own indicators of how the Hebrew Bible was to be pronounced, the Jewish Masoretes were providing their own interpretation of the various words. They were not inspired individuals, and at times their efforts fell short. All in all, they produced a remarkably accurate rendition, but in numerous places our modern English translations have chosen to depart from the Masoretic reading of the Hebrew consonantal text when doing so was warranted by context and/or linguistic evidence. In the case of the Prayer of Jabez, such a departure is also justified, in my view. Perhaps future translations will take the evidence presented here into consideration.

Breaking the key line down into the basic Hebrew words/segments:

"And make" + "from evil/harm" +
"so as not to" + "distress/pain me" =
"And keep (?) me (supplied by context)
from evil/harm so as not to distress/pain me."

The main snag remains the alleged "keep me from evil" as a way for us to render the Hebrew verb 'ASAH, normally translated as "do, make, provide, prepare." The three arguably most important ancient translation traditions that we possess—the Greek Septuagint, the Latin Vulgate, and the Aramaic Targum—*all* opt for some form of "make" or "provide" in their translations. Only in the Syriac Peshitta, the Christian Aramaic translation of the Eastern Church, do we find the translation "keep from, separate from" (Aramaic PRQ) for this passage. As we will soon see, the Peshitta had a number of interesting twists when it came to this passage. Of all the ancient translations, the Syriac Peshitta is the most unusual and the most confused.

I have argued earlier that the connection between the last word of the prayer meaning "pain me" ('OTSBI) and the RA'AH word meaning "harm, evil" was too tempting for the Jewish Masoretes to pass up on. This led them far off the correct path, the one that recognizes that the RA'AH, "shepherd, pasture," root is instead involved.

6. The Jewish Targum (Aramaic translation)

In general, Chronicles received marginal attention in Judaism. (But when they did give it their attention, things got interesting, as we shall see!) There are only a couple of manuscripts of the Targum of Chronicles that scholars are aware of, and several prominent ancient Jewish sages wrongly contended that there was no such thing as a Targum for Chronicles. The manuscript that was used in the standard edition of the Targum by Alexander Sperber (*The Bible in Aramaic*, [Brill], 1959–) is quite late, coming from the 9th century A. D.

So what is a Targum? Basically the term refers to the Aramaic translation of the Old Testament produced by various Jewish scholars through the centuries. When the Jews were taken into the Babylonian captivity some 600 years before Christ, they came to learn and use Aramaic even more than Hebrew. Because it was much more "user friendly" than the cuneiform Assyrian and Babylonian languages, Aramaic had come to be the official diplomatic language during the Assyrian and Babylonian empires. (The term "cuneiform" refers to the "wedge" [Latin *cuneus*] shapes made in writing these languages with a stylus on soft clay tablets. Some 500 signs, ranging widely in complexity, were involved.)

Aramaic and Hebrew are closely related languages, so the jump was not a difficult one for the Jews to make. Both languages use the very same letters, and the vocabulary and grammar are quite similar. By the time of Ezra and Nehemiah (possibly the time during which Chronicles was penned), the Jews in Jerusalem already spoke Aramaic more commonly than Hebrew. Nehemiah 8:8 seems to suggest that when Ezra read to the people from the Law, select men translated into Aramaic so that the populace could understand what was being said. The Jewish population, immediately after the return from captivity and for centuries to come, employed Aramaic as the language of choice. Hebrew was of course also preserved, especially among the more educated.

The date for the Targums of the individual Old Testament books is hard to determine. We can assume that the process of translating a number of these books into Aramaic was done early on, since an obvious need existed. We have a pre-Christian copy of the Targum of Job that was discovered among the Dead Sea Scrolls. One could argue that if there was felt a need to translate a book like Job, other books must have been translated into Aramaic at an early stage. Some of Leviticus in Aramaic is also known from that early time.

Most of the surviving Targums have material in them that seems to come from a range of periods—they were works in process to which successive scribes added further material. One of the most important things to recognize is that many Targums were not strict translations or even paraphrases, but rather were interpretive renderings that we might classify more as commentaries. In general, the Pentateuch or Law of Moses was treated in a more literal fashion than other books. Chronicles, on the other hand, was handled in a highly interpretative way, a way which appears strange to most Christians. Let's see what they did. Words in brackets are actually a part of their "translation," but are obviously not based on the original Hebrew text.

The Jewish Targum of "The Prayer of Jabez"

Now Jabez [who is Othniel] was honored [and wise in the Law] more than his brothers. And his mother called his name Ya'bets because she bore him in pain. And Ya'bets prayed to the God of Israel, saying: "Would that You indeed bless me [with sons] and enlarge my territory [with students]. And may your hand be with me [in negotiations]. And may you provide me with close ("like-minded") companions so that evil desire might not "stir" me. And the LORD brought about what he asked for. (my translation)

The following brief notes are being supplied to help in understanding the wording of the Jewish Targum.

1. **"Ya'bets"** is closer to the actual pronunciation of the name.

2. **"Who is Othniel."** The following chapter will more fully develop the Jewish treatment of Jabez. In their speculative approach, "Jabez" is viewed as being

another name for Othniel, the first judge in Israel (Judges 1:12-15; 2:7-11). Once this road is taken, Jabez's "career" really takes off!

3. **"And wise in the Law."** These words would seem to be an attempt to explain why Jabez/Othniel was honored. Jewish tradition portrays Jabez as a great teacher of the Law, again with no real Scriptural basis.

4. **"Bless me with sons and enlarge my territory with students."** Since Jabez is viewed as a great ancient "Rabbi" in Judaism, the desire for "sons" and "students" makes sense. It's just not what Jabez actually prayed for.

5. **"May your hand be with me in negotiations."** The expression "in negotiations" is a paraphrase of the Jewish idiom "in weighing and shaking"—terms apparently dealing with the marketplace.

6. **"Provide me with companions"** the Targum translates. We see here the attempt to render yet *another* RA'AH root in Hebrew—"friend, companion"! Hebrew and related languages, like Aramaic or Arabic, have a rather striking feature. Nearly all Hebrew verb roots are *triliteral*—made up of three and only three root letters. This makes learning vocabulary a bit more of a challenge. Just think of lists and lists of words, all containing various combinations of just three letters. Admittedly, not a pretty sight.

The Targum translates the supposed word "companions" with a standard Aramaic term for "friends, companions," KHABRAYYA.

7. **"So that evil desire might not stir me."** This seems to be their way of rendering both the original MR'H, reading "from evil," together with the phrase "so as not to pain me." But note that they have *already* utilized the word MR'H in their translation "close companions." This was a frequent interpretative technique employed by the translators of the Targum at times—allowing a key word to serve double duty.

I've gone into some detail here on the Targum on the Prayer of Jabez. Very few Christians have ever heard of the Jewish Targum. Almost none have seen its rendition of the Prayer of Jabez. I hope this has been more enlightening than bewildering. One thing should be clear from this, however. Modern speculations are mild compared to what the ancient Jewish sages did on behalf of Jabez! More to come in the section on "Rabbi Jabez."

7. The Eastern Christian "Peshitta" (Syriac [Christian Aramaic] translation, c. 6-7th century).

The Eastern Syrian Church has a rich literary heritage that is not well-known by the modern church. Part of this heritage was the Peshitta, the Syriac (Christian Aramaic) translation of the Bible. The Syrian church bore the brunt of the early spread of Islam and its influence thus diminished greatly. The Peshitta bears witness to this eastern branch's early contribution to Christianity.

The Peshitta is highly interpretative at this passage regarding Jabez, much like some of the Jewish Targums in general. We ought to note that for these early Christians, the passage as we have it in our Masoretic Text had some "problems." Or let's just say the interpreters perhaps had a few issues that they may have sought to resolve, such as:

(1) The account concerning Jabez is not connected with anything before or after it.

(2) Where's Jabez's *father*?

(3) Do we need to talk about all that "pain in childbirth" stuff?

(4) Isn't Jabez a crummy name, anyway?

(5) Doesn't this prayer have a selfish ring to it?

The highly respected Peshitta did a real number to the "Prayer of Jabez":

The Syriac Peshitta of "The Prayer of Jabez"

Now Ahishur the father of Tekoa had two wives, and one of them gave birth to Ahiram and Tepher and Temen and Harashtar. These were the sons of one of them. Now one of the sons was dear to his father and mother. And he (his father) called his name 'Aynay ("my eyes"). And he said to him: "May the Lord indeed bless you. And may He expand your territory, and may His hand be with you. May He keep you from evil so that it may

not have power over you. And may He give you whatever you ask of Him." (my translation)

Not having an English translation of the Peshitta readily available at the time, I needed to translate the Syriac on my own. Thought it would take just a few minutes to figure what was going on. Right away, however, I knew I was in trouble.

The line of the prayer that was supposed to read "and may your hand be with me" instead read "and may HIS hand be with YOU"! Something was awry here. Apparently this wasn't the prayer of Jabez at all, but of someone else. I assumed it must have been Jabez's parent(s). A quick scan of the preceding lines confirmed this. Before proceeding here with the discussion, it might be good to put this particular Peshitta passage into some overall context for your consideration. (The only translation of the Peshitta available in English today is that of George M. Lamsa, *Holy Bible: From the Ancient Eastern Text*, HarperCollins Publishers. He chooses to loosely render the "he" referring to the father as "they," thus making the prayer offered by both parents. The text literally reads as singular, "he.")

Two major issues or problems are converging in the Syriac rendition of the Prayer of Jabez. One is the issue of translation technique or system. In general, the Syrac Peshitta is a quite literal, accurate ancient translation of the Hebrew Scriptures. BUT NOT IN CHRONICLES! The Peshitta of Chronicles is quite distinctive in its loose translation practice, a practice similar to, but not quite identical to, the targumic or Rabbinic practices found in Judaism. Scholars still debate whether or not the Christian Syriac translation of Chronicles actually preserves an ancient Jewish Targum. (See now Michael P. Weitzman, "Is the Peshitta of Chronicles a Targum?" in *Targum Studies, Vol. II*, Paul V. M. Flesher, ed., [Scholars Press, 1998] , pp. 159-193.) The bottom line is that our Prayer of Jabez occurs in a section of the Peshitta that can be expected to give an expanded, interpretive rendering. Our expectations are more than met!

The other key issue involved here is the status of the Hebrew text utilized by the translator(s) of the Syriac Peshitta for Chronicles. Many scholars believe that a worn, corrupted Hebrew manuscript was employed by the Peshitta of Chronicles. A number of sections suggest that Hebrew words were missing or misread, the latter possibly because of partial obliteration of various letters. (See Weitzman's article for details.) IT SO HAPPENS THAT THE GROUP OF LINES IMMEDIATELY PRECEDING THE PRAYER OF JABEZ IS SUCH A SECTION.

What we find preceding Jabez's prayer is that our verses 7-8 are missing in the Peshitta. The information found in verses 5-6 is merged with that in verses 9-10. Thus we "learn" the name of Jabez's father–Ahishur. But, surprisingly, we find ourselves missing a rather important name, that of Jabez himself! Instead the name 'Aynay, "my eyes," is given as a second name for one of the four sons mentioned earlier. There's just no "Jabez"! As stated above, some have argued that the available Hebrew manuscript was defective here and contributed to the confusion. But in truth, we do not fully understand all the contributing factors causing the dramatic differences found in the Peshitta of Chronicles. (As a parallel, we note that a few verses later, I Chronicles 4:15-18, some thirty names in the Masoretic Text of the Hebrew Bible are reduced to just *six* in the Peshitta, all referred to as the sons of Caleb.)

The following equations display the differences in rather basic terms. Several different textual problems may have been involved. Specialists who are interested can further investigate the details.

1. "And it came about that Jabez" = "And one of them"

(The text must have been partially obliterated.)

2. "Honored more than his brothers. And his mother called him . . . ." = "Dear to his father and his mother. And he called him . . . ."

(Probably key here is that the words "his brothers" and "his father" look very similar.)

3. "Ya'bets" = 'Aynay ("my eyes")
(*Was the original text partly obliterated?*)

4. Jabez speaks = Jabez's *father* speaks
(*Therefore "you," etc. [God] = "he," etc; while "me,"*
etc. [Jabez] = "you.")

5. The phrase, "saying 'Because I bore him in pain,'" may have been omitted due to a scribal slip. The words "Jabez" and "in pain" looked similar. The scribes eyes, therefore, may have skipped over from the one to the other, in the process leaving out the above phrase. The inadvertent skipping of words or phrases this way is a well-known scribal phenomenon (present also today in modern term papers!).

Enough of textual details. The essence of all this is that the Peshitta text in no way resembles what the Hebrew originally said. Jabez's mother's statement regarding pain in childbirth is *gone*. Jabez's *father* actually prays "the prayer." Jabez's name is gone, replaced by the name 'Aynay, "my eyes." The statement that God granted

> **In the Peshitta version of the ancient Eastern Syrian church, it is actually Jabez's father who prays the now-famous prayer!**

the request is instead expressed as a wish: "may He grant you whatever you ask for." In sum, the translators of the

Peshitta didn't get much right here. Note that they *did* concur with the conventional understanding of MR'H as representing MERA'AH, "from evil." But as I have tried to demonstrate, they didn't get that right either!

8. Summary

The Greek Septuagint, the Latin Vulgate, the Masoretic pointed Hebrew text, the Jewish Aramaic Targum, the Eastern Christian Syriac Peshitta — the key witnesses to the original Hebrew Bible — none of these conveyed the original content of the Prayer of Jabez. What I have called "The Lost Prayer of Jabez" really *was* "lost" all these many centuries. But once the idea that W'SYT MR'H means "and provide me with pasture land" is accepted, once Jabez's "Lost Prayer" is "found," a lot of translation and interpretation problems get considerably easier.

Many of the articles and books now being published in "rebuttal" of Bruce Wilkinson's application of "The Prayer of Jabez" make good points, BUT THEY MISS THE MAIN ISSUE—HOW CHRISTIANS SHOULD TAKE WHAT JABEZ ORIGINALLY PRAYED AND APPLY IT TO THEIR LIVES TODAY. The key here is "WHAT JABEZ *ORIGINALLY* PRAYED." False assumptions made by scores of recent Christian writers on "Jabez" have rendered their treatments pretty much irrelevant. Once you replace the words "And keep me from evil" with "And provide me with pasture land," the discussion is pretty well over, isn't it? Well, *isn't it?*

"Rabbi Jabez" and the Jewish Sages

By now I hope that you have become convinced of the main thesis of this book. When it comes to what Jabez actually prayed, just about everyone seems to have missed the boat. This section now on "Rabbi Jabez" is the exclamation point. It demonstrates that ancient Jewish interpreters also went far beyond what the Biblical text concerning Jabez could ever warrant. In fact, what is going on in Christian circles today seems tame in comparison.

Our analysis of the Targum's rendering in the previous section illustrated that the ancient Jewish Sages went to quite an extreme in spiritualizing the Prayer of Jabez. We now want to put this in a broader setting so that you can see the full scope of how Jabez was treated in ancient Judaism. Before doing so, a little background may be needed.

The Origins of the Jewish Sages

Most of what is referred to today as "Judaism" follows the path of Rabbinic Judaism. The term "Rabbinic" is based on the word "Rabbi" or "Teacher." What many Christians do not realize is that the spiritual ancestors of Rabbinic Judaism were the Pharisees of Jesus' day.

The Pharisees and the Sadducees represented two of the mainstream Jewish parties in the first century. Their beginnings went farther back than that, however. The Old Testament mentions neither; their origin dates to the time between the close of the Old Testament record and the opening of the new era announced in the Gospel accounts. They are mentioned at length by the Jewish historian Josephus. The earliest historical mention of the Pharisees and Sadducees is from the reign of the Jewish Hasmonean King John Hyrcanus, 134-104 B.C. (For a useful survey of the history of the "Time Between the Testaments," try F. F. Bruce, *Israel and the Nations* [Eerdmans, 1969].) These earlier records depict in even greater detail than the New Testament the power struggle that positioned the Pharisaic and Sadducean parties against one another.

Since the Sadducees were more directly tied to the priesthood and the temple administration, their party effectively ended with the fall of Jerusalem and the destruction of the temple in A.D. 70. With the demise of the Sadducees (literally the "set-apart ones"), the Pharisees (literally the "separated ones") no longer needed a distinctive title. In our day, the United States generally embraces a two-party system: Republicans and Democrats. If one party (you choose) were to become defunct, what would be left would be . . . Americans! Similarly, with the Sadducees no longer in business, the Pharisees become known simply as the "Rabbis." Pharisaic Judaism becomes "Rabbinic" Judaism.

The "Oral Law" and the Jewish Sages

Most Christians do not understand the magnitude of the remarkable "revolution" introduced by Pharisaic Judaism. The exact genesis of this revolution is buried in the murky waters of ancient religious history, probably never to be fully understood. But the product of their efforts has had far-reaching effects.

In a nutshell, the Pharisees promoted an authoritative body of dogma know as the "Oral Law." The Oral Law is what the Gospels refer to as the "traditions of the elders" (Mark 7:3-5). Confrontations between Jesus and the Pharisees were not over issues of interpreting the Old Testament Law as much as they were the Oral Law. Things like various ritual washings, picking grain on the Sabbath ("work"!), healing on the Sabbath (*more* "work"!)—these were regulations spelled out in the Oral Law of the Pharisees, *not* in the pages of Old Testament Scripture.

The Oral Law was an ingenious invention by the Pharisees, for it allowed them to exercise religious control over the masses—Jews who in fact bought into this notion of the authoritative Oral Law. In essence, the Pharisees claimed that when Moses was up on Mt. Sinai, he received *two* laws: one *written*, the other *oral*. Allegedly, this latter Oral Law was handed down by world of mouth through great leaders of the Old Testament, culminating centuries later in the efforts of the important scribe Ezra and a religious body (shrouded in mystery) known as the "Great Synagogue." With this, we are now roughly at the close of Old Testament history. The subsequent Pharisees claimed to be ultimate custodians of this long-preserved Oral Law. In reality, they were its inventors.

The minute regulations and practices imbedded in this Oral Law no doubt arose from a felt need in Jewish society. The Old Testament Law was not viewed as sufficiently precise and relevant to legislate the later metropolitan and economically diversified Jewish society. The genius of the Pharisaic "revolution" can be seen clearly in two important areas. (1) The Pharisees were able to convince the people that the Oral Law was equal to the written in importance. It could not be ignored. (2) They kept it "oral" for several centuries. Only the "scribes and Pharisees" had mastery over this material. The only way you could be sure you were on the right track was to go to the religious authorities — the Pharisees themselves.

Typically in the Oral Law, various earlier Rabbis would be quoted on some of the finer points. In fact various Pharisaic schools disagreed on some issues. The "school of Hillel" and the "school of Shammai" are names of famous competitors known from the first Christian century. Often the laws would say "Rabbi X says such and such, but Rabbi Y says . . . ." Jesus' appeal to his own divine authority stood in such contrast to the typical religious argument of his day. No wonder "the crowds were amazed at his teaching, because he taught as one who had authority, and not as their teachers of the law" (Matthew 7:28-29).

The bottom line for us to keep in mind is that the Oral Law was viewed as binding upon the Jews in their attempts to follow God's revealed will. The majority of the Jews of Jesus' day embraced this claim. The Pharisaic revolution was indeed a great "success."

The Writings of the Jewish Sages

Most of the great literature in Judaism is to be attributed to the work of the Rabbinic Sages. Although originally the "Oral" Law, eventually the voluminous deliberations and findings of the Rabbis were put into written form (ca. A.D. 200). This document was known as the MISHNAH ("Repetition"). As the Rabbis continued to pontificate, their law code grew to incorporate further commentary on the Mishnah itself. The combination of the two came to be known as the TALMUD. Although the translated Mishnah has been published as a single-volume work (e.g., Danby's), the Talmud is a massive repository of Jewish law and lore, encompassing many volumes (roughly A.D. 300-600). The Talmud is divided into 63 sections known as "tractates." Regarding our study of Jabez, tractate *Temurah* ("Substitution") takes on special significance.

For the most part, the various TARGUMIM were the work of the Rabbis, and like the Talmud, they spanned several centuries. As noted earlier, the Targum was an Aramaic translation that, to differing degrees, incorporated elements of interpretation and commentary built right into the "translation" itself. The Targum of Chronicles was particularly loose and expansionistic in its treatment.

Along with the Mishnah, Talmud and Targum, we must also note the commentaries on Old Testament books known as the MIDRASHIM. The term "Midrash" comes from the Hebrew root meaning to "seek (the meaning)," or "interpret." Jewish Midrash, however is noted for its tendency to insert or *add* "meaning" to the text, not to derive it from the text itself. (Christian interpreters often contrast the terms "exegesis" [getting something *out of* a passage] and "eisegesis" [reading something *into* a passage].) Many of the midrashic treatments are fanciful, forced and, at times, even funny. They generally offer little help in ascertaining what the *original* meaning of a passage may have been.

The following treatment of Jabez according to the Jewish sages incorporates in the main the views expressed in the Rabbinic writings: Mishnah and Talmud, Midrash and Targum. It would be extremely unwieldy and counter productive to offer point-by-point citations for the descriptions to follow. Instead, here are the key sources consulted.

(1) *Hebrew-English Edition of the Babylonian Talmud. Temurah.* Trans. with notes, glossary and indices by Rabbi L. Miller. Rabbi Dr. I. Epstein, ed. Soncino, 1989.

(2) *divrei hayamim I (I Chronicles). A New Translation with a Commentary Anthologized from Talmudic, Midrashic and Rabbinic Sources. Translation and Commentary* by Rabbi Moshe Eisemann. *Overviews* by Rabbi Moshe Eisemann *with* Rabbi Nosson Scherman. *Edited* by Rabbi Yehezkel Danziger. Mesorah Publications, 1987.

(3) *I Chronicles. A New English Translation.*
Translation of Text, Rashi and Commentary by Rabbi
A. J. Rosenberg. The Judaic Press, 1992.

(4) *The Targum of Chronicles.* Translated with
Introduction, and notes, by J. Stanley McIvor. This was
published along with *The Targum of Ruth* by D. R. G.
Beattie. Liturgical Press, 1994.

English translations of the Targum to Chronicles
are hard to come by, so McIvor's work is especially useful.
Every Christian seminary should get a hold of the *divrei
hayamim* volume as well. All in all, the picture painted
in the ancient documents that were produced by the
Jewish Sages opens up a whole new, somewhat
bewildering, world for Christian students of the Bible.

Chronicles and the Jewish Sages

One of the basic Rabbinic tenets of interpreting
Scripture was modified when it came to Chronicles. The
Sages generally recognized two principles of
interpretation: the *peshat*, or "simple meaning," and the
derash, or "homiletical elucidation." However,
according to the commentary on Leviticus (*Leviticus
Rabbah*), the Book of Chronicles was only to receive
the *homiletical* treatment. The *peshat*, based on what
the text literally meant, was bypassed. This sets up Jabez
for a real makeover, as you might guess.

A revealing statement from the Sages concerns the section of I Chronicles between 8:38 and 9:44 (a portion of genealogies beginning and ending with the name "Azel"). According to the Talmud (*Pesachim* 62b), to expound upon these verses between the two "Azels," "we would need 400 camel-loads of exegetical interpretations!" All that for a list of names?

One of the prominent features of the Sages' approach to Chronicles was to apply more than one name from the genealogies to a famous individual. As a classic example, a bit farther down from Jabez's prayer in I Chronicles 4, at verse eighteen, six names given there are applied to *Moses*, using arguments based on meanings allegedly related to the specific names. The names are Jered, Gedor, Heber, Soco, Jekuthiel, and Zanoah. It is stated, for example, that Moses was called Jered "because he brought down manna for Israel" (Targum at 4:18). The name "Jered" is based on the root YARAD, "to go down," hence the connection. Of course, none of these names in the genealogical list at I Chronicles 4:18 actually have *anything* to do with Moses.

"Rabbi Jabez" and the Jewish Sages

SO WHAT ABOUT *JABEZ*? Quite a picture of Jabez emerges at the hands of the Jewish Sages. Let's enumerate the key steps in the development of the Rabbinic portrait of "Rabbi Jabez."

1. According to the Sages, many hundreds of points of law were forgotten in the mourning period immediately following the death of Moses (some 1,700 legal rulings, according to the Talmud [*Temurah* 16a]). Joshua forgot many of the laws, the Sages maintained, but fortunately they were restored by Israel's first judge, Othniel.

2. The Sages then identified Othniel with Jabez! According to *Temurah* 16a again, one early Rabbi taught: "Othniel is the same as Jabez. He was called Othniel ('OTNI'EL) because God ('EL) answered him ('ANAH), and Jabez (YA'BETS) because he counselled (YA'ATS) and fostered Torah in Israel." (Often the Sages connected names with verbal roots that showed only superficial similarity to them.) In two "easy" steps, Jabez had been transformed by the Sages into one of the greatest teachers of the Law Israel ever had.

In accordance with such an approach, one of the most famous Rabbis of all, Rabbi Judah the Prince (credited with leading the effort to produce the written Mishnah, A.D. 200) gave the following rendering of Jabez's prayer (additions in brackets):

If thou wouldst bless me indeed [*by multiplying and increasing*]; and enlarge my border [*with sons and daughters*]; and that thine hand might be with me [*in business*]; and thou wouldst keep me from evil [*that I have no head-ache, ear-ache, nor eye-ache*]; that it may not grieve me, [*that the evil inclination may not have power over me so as to prevent me from studying.*

120

If thou doest so, it is well; but if not, I will go with my 'grief' to the grave]. **And God granted him that which he requested. (*Temurah* 16a)**

We have already documented the rendering of the Aramaic Targum, in which Jabez prayed both for numerous children and disciples. He also sought the godly influence of "close companions" who would help him resist evil, at least according to the Targum.

3. Now an obscure comment in I Chronicles 2:55 comes into play. There we read about "the clans of scribes who lived at Jabez." This is the only other use of the name "Jabez" outside of I Chronicles 4:9-10. Here, however, it seems to refer to a *place*, not a person. At least that's how the verse has generally been understood. But some of the Rabbis saw things differently. They equated the two "Jabezes" and therefore read at 2:55 "the scribes *of* Jabez," that is, his disciples. Now we have Jabez running a scribal school, teaching the Law of Moses to willing disciples.

4. Among the other names mentioned in I Chronicles 2:55 we find reference to the Kenites and the Rechabites ("house of Rechab"). Let's tackle the Kenites first.

Through the mention of the Kenites at I Chronicles 2:55, the Sages could connect Jabez (Othniel) with the descendants of Moses' father-in-law Jethro. No proselyte ever loved the Torah Law as much as Jethro did, according to the Sages. And Jethro's children loved the Torah, too. That's why they left Jericho and went down to the Desert of Judah (Judges 1:16)—in order to hook up with Rabbi Jabez and be taught by him. This was in answer to Jabez's prayer, of course. Jabez prayed for students. The Kenites needed a teacher. And the rest is Rabbinic history.

5. The mention of the house of Rechab enabled the Sages to make another alleged connection with Jabez. The Rechabites were a unique family that lived on the fringe of Israelite society. Their ancestor Jonadab had made them swear a vow of abstinence from wine and from a life of sedentary dwelling. They were to be a separate people, living as nomads in tents (Jeremiah 35). In Jeremiah's day, the Rechabites served as an example of obedience and faithfulness to their "father," an example not followed by most of the Jews of that time in reference to the laws of their heavenly Father.

According to the Sages, as a reward to the Rechabites, Jabez was given to them as a teacher of the Law. The names Tirathites, Shimeathites and Sucathites at I Chronicles 2:55 are all held to be descriptions or names of the Rechabites. As scribes they sat at the gate (TERA'; Tirathites=TIR'ATIM), listening to their father's commands (SHAMA', "hear"; Shimeathites= SHIM'ATIM) and living in huts (SAKAK, "cast shade"; Sucathites = SUKATIM). Once again, connections with various Hebrew words and names are made as an interpretive device.

The picture is now complete. By a series of highly unlikely connections, the Jewish Sages transformed Jabez into an ancient Rabbi who functioned not only as the first judge of Israel (Othniel), but also as the rescuer of many laws lost after the death of Moses! He ran a scribal school in the Desert of Judah and taught the descendants of Moses' father-in-law Jethro, as well as the early Rechabite clan. A fascinating tale, wouldn't you say?

What does this ancient Jewish portrait of Jabez tell us about the *real* Jabez of Old Testament Scripture? Nothing, really. But, based upon our earlier "discovery," you already knew that.

Imagine how different the "history" of the Prayer of Jabez would have been had the original status of the word MIR'EH, "pasture land," been preserved correctly in later generations. Bye, bye "Rabbi Jabez."

The current Jabez fascination has a long, if not well-known, pedigree. Modern Christians have gone overboard in their attempts to spiritualize Jabez and his words. Ancient Jews, however even exceeded these recent efforts. They just didn't have the Jabez prayer shawls and CD's and song books and Bible covers and devotional diaries and key chains and T-shirts and wall plaques and . . . .

A Final Word for Specialists

Without wishing to complicate the matter further, for the sake of completeness I wish to call your attention to two important articles that impact the Prayer of Jabez discussion.

The first is by D. Winton Thomas, and it appeared in *The Bible Translator*, Vol. 17 (October, 1966), pp. 190-193 ("Translating Hebrew 'ĀSĀH"). Thomas argues that a number of instances involving the Hebrew root 'ĀSĀH do not fit the normal meanings understood for that root. He suggests that in such instances we should seek another root, citing several Arabic roots that might provide us with comparative evidence.

Thomas suggests two possible Arabic roots, GHASHĀ, meaning "cover, conceal," and 'ASHĀ, meaning "turn." He offers some fifteen passages where he thinks that these other meanings might make more sense. Upon closer examination, however, the majority of Thomas's examples are far from persuasive.

In the case of Jabez's prayer, Thomas suggests the rendering "and thou turnest thyself from evil so as not to vex me." Turning away from evil is something that God often asks His wicked people to do (using verbs like SHUB and SUR for this). I'm not sure how the idea of *us requesting God to turn away from evil* should work. Any thoughts?

The idea of "cover me from evil," which on the surface might sound plausible, is not a tidy solution either. The common Biblical Hebrew word for "cover, conceal, KISSAH, does not present the meaning of "protect someone from X." The supposed examples that Thomas has dug up regarding 'ASAH do not convey the idea of "protect" or "keep from" either. In fact, of the ten proposed examples of "to cover," only one or two are at all convincing.

One big strike against this approach in connection with Jabez's prayer is that generally prayers are expressed in *predictable*, often *formulaic* language. Rare words don't usually surface unless they are paired in tight parallelism with more common ones.

Thomas's approach in general is suggestive, but in my view it does not relate to the Prayer of Jabez at all, regardless of how it may or may not fit in other specific instances.

My conclusion? We should stick with the meaning of 'ASAH known in the 2,600 or so examples we have in the Old Testament, and with the obvious contextual ties we have in this passage that indicate that our word here is not MERA'AH, "from evil," but rather MIR'EH, "pasture land."

The second article to be noted is a recent one by R. Christopher Heard, professor at Milligan College

(Milligan College, TN), entitled "Echoes of Genesis in 1 Chronicles 4:9-10: An Intertextual and Contextual Reading of Jabez's Prayer" (*The Journal of Hebrew Scriptures*, Vol. 4: Article 2 [2002]). I was made aware of the upcoming publication of this article by the author during correspondence related to the publication of the first edition of my *The Lost Prayer of Jabez*. Professor Heard graciously acknowledges my book within the footnotes of his article.

We learned that each of us had concluded that MIR'EH was the best reading of the form in Jabez's prayer. Heard also argues at length against Thomas' approach regarding the meaning of 'ASAH at I Chronicles 4:10, confirming my own conclusions. Consult his work for details. His fine article is highly technical, being geared to Hebrew specialists. To my knowledge, Professor Heard and I are the only authors who have argued the case for the reading "pasture land" in the Prayer of Jabez.

For information about obtaining
The Lost Prayer of Jabez,

go to

www.lostjabez.com

or write

MIREH Publishers
P. O. Box 1376
Joplin, MO 64802

In order to send a friend a "peek"
regarding what this book is all about,
you can go to the *lostjabez.com* link called
"From Jabez With Regrets."
What better way to get the scoop
than to read a letter from Jabez himself?!
This amusing letter can be directly e-mailed
from there to interested parties.